Happy
Birthday
Julie
2016
♡ Betsy

100 jams, jellies, preserves & pickles

100 jams, jellies, preserves & pickles

recipes and techniques for preserving fruits and vegetables

GLORIA NICOL
The Laundry

CICO BOOKS
LONDON NEW YORK

*For my mum, Alice Nicol, for her
unconditional love, help, and support,
without which I would be lost.*

First published in 2009 by CICO Books as
Fruits of the Earth
This paperback edition published in 2011
by CICO Books
an imprint of Ryland Peters & Small Ltd
519 Broadway, 5th Floor, New York,
NY 10012
www.cicobooks.com

10 9 8 7 6 5 4 3 2 1

Text copyright © Gloria Nicol 2009, 2011
Design, photography, and illustration
copyright © CICO Books 2009, 2011

A CIP catalog record for this book is
available from the Library of Congress.

Paperback ISBN: 978-1-907563-90-4
(Hardback ISBN: 978-1-906525-27-9)

Printed in China

Project Editor: Gillian Haslam
Text Editors: Alison Bolus and
                    Eleanor Van Zandt
Designer: Barbara Zuñiga
Photographer: Gloria Nicol
Illustrator: Jane Smith
Stylist: Sue Rowlands
(Pages 93, 95, 120, and 125: photographer
Winfried Heinze; stylist Rose Hammick)

contents

why make jam?

There is something so satisfying about opening a food cabinet or pantry to find the shelves stacked with colorful jars of homemade preserves. These containers of summer and fall flavors might be just what's required to lift the mood on a dark, gloomy winter's day, when a good dollop of strawberry jam on your bread reminds you of longer, warmer, lighter days. For me, that is what making preserves is all about: capturing the essence of whatever fruit or vegetable it is and sealing that flavor in a jar for another day.

I started making jam 30 or so years ago and have always enjoyed it, despite my fair share of sticky mistakes. It is a traditional part of homemaking that celebrates the seasons and somehow makes life cozier and more comforting. My preserves are handmade and full of chunky pieces, which sets them apart from anything store-bought. The flavors of the fruits shine through and are rarely masked with spices. Where possible, I reduce the amount of sugar, because the tarter the fruits, the fresher tasting the results.

In the current climate of concerns about being less wasteful, clocking up fewer food miles and eating seasonal, locally grown food, making preserves has never been so popular.

choosing your ingredients

Although strawberries—to give just one example—can now be bought virtually all year round, thanks to the introduction of new varieties, the use of field tunnels, and the massive increase in imported produce, nothing beats the flavor of a homegrown strawberry that has ripened in the sun and been picked only moments before. It is this flavor, so sweet and intense, that can be captured in preserves.

Using your own homegrown produce for preserving is hard to beat, because the ingredients will be fresh and you will have control over their growing conditions.

Farmers' markets are another great source. You'll know that the fruit and vegetables have been grown locally, and you are more likely to find unusual varieties. Whatever its source, rinse produce before use, although ideally not bush fruits since rinsing can reduce their juice content. However, if they may have been sprayed, you will need to rinse and drain them.

Food for free

Sometimes ingredients are right in front of your nose, and all you have to do is go out there and find them. Woodlands and hedgerows (if you live in a part of the country where these are common) are full of edible fruits and berries if you know what to look for. You may find crab apples growing wild, along with damsons, greengages, or blackberries. Alternatively, if you know someone who grows more fruit than they can use, offer to take it off their hands in exchange for a jar of preserve made using it. It's a win-win situation.

Fruit and pectin

For almost all fruit preserves you need to choose fresh, good-quality, just-ripe fruit in order to achieve the correct pectin content. This is because jam needs the right balance of pectin, acid, and sugar to set properly. Different fruits contain varying amounts of pectin, and the pectin content is higher in just-ripe fruit. Fruits high

in pectin include crab apples, Seville oranges, damsons, gooseberries, quinces, and currants. Fruits low in pectin include strawberries, pears, elderberries, fresh apricots, and cherries. Some fruits contain very little pectin, and so jams made using these fruits will need additional help to make them set. Overripe fruit can also lower the pectin content, which is why such fruit is not suitable for jams. It is, however, suitable for nectars, so use any fruit that is too ripe for jam to make a delicious nectar or syrup.

The pectin content can be raised in various ways. Mixed-fruit jams can use the higher pectin content of one fruit to offset the lower content of another; lemon juice can be added at a rate of the juice of 1–2 lemons to every 4 pounds of fruit, or bottled pectin can be used.

preserving equipment

The principle underlying all preserving is to prevent decay caused by the growth of yeasts, molds, and bacteria. These organisms are destroyed when heated to sufficiently high temperatures to sterilize them, and, once sterilized, preserves must be kept securely sealed so that air cannot enter. Preserves that contain 60 percent or more of sugar are less susceptible to the growth of yeasts, which is why jams containing less sugar need to be eaten more quickly.

THE JARS

The jars normally used for preserving in the United States are called mason jars. They have a screw-on lid consisting of two or more sections to help ensure a tight seal. You may also find European-style canning jars, which have glass tops, secured by a thick wire clamp. Both types come in a range of sizes.

You can also use recycled jam or other condiment jars. Make sure, however, that the jars have no chips or cracks and that the lids fit securely. Corrosive materials must not come into contact with the preserve, especially if it contains vinegar (as used in chutneys and pickles), so make sure that the lids will not corrode.

The jars must be sterilized and the simple method I prefer is as follows. Wash the jars in hot soapy water, rinse in hot water, and leave to air-dry. Place a folded dish towel on an oven shelf and lay the jars on their sides on top. Shortly before you need to use them, heat the oven to 225°F, and leave the jars at this temperature for 30 minutes. The jars should still be hot when you fill them with hot jam.

OTHER SPECIAL EQUIPMENT

There are a few items you can buy for preserving:

PRESERVING PAN   A noncorrosive, nonreactive preserving pan, big enough to hold large quantities of boiling jam, is a great investment. This type of pan is wide and shallow to encourage rapid evaporation when bringing jam to setting point. A good-quality pan will have a thick, heavy base, which will prevent any preserve from burning. While copper and aluminum pans are both popular, I think stainless steel is best, and it is certainly necessary when making preserves that contain vinegar.

When jam is brought to a rolling boil, it rises up in the pan, so never over-fill the pan. If the pan is too small and overfilled, you will either end up with an overflowing mess of boiling syrupy jam or, in order to prevent this happening, you won't be able to raise the temperature high enough to reach setting point.

DOUBLE BOILER   Useful when making fruit curds and fruit syrups and nectars, this can, however, be replaced by a bowl set over a pan of simmering water.

FOOD MILL A good-quality food mill with several disks of various degrees of coarseness can be used to sieve fruit to extract the purée, which is excellent for making jams and gives a pleasing texture. You can purée apples without having to peel and core them first.

JAR FUNNEL This is essential for pouring hot jam safely into jars. Choose one small enough to fit into most of your jars but wide enough not to become clogged with pieces of fruit. Sterilize and warm the funnel in the oven along with the jars. A sterilized, warmed scoop is useful for ladling jam into the funnel.

JAR LIFTER Special tongs, called a jar lifter, are used for handling the hot jars.

JAM THERMOMETER Although not essential, this is useful for testing for setting point. Choose one that goes up to at least 230°F and has a clip to attach it to the side of the pan.

JELLY BAG Ready-made jelly bags in a plastic stand that will fit over a bowl are ideal for straining the juices from cooked fruit, but you could make your own using muslin, nylon, a clean tea towel, or unbleached muslin tied across the legs of an upturned stool.

MUSLIN You will need squares of muslin to hold stones and spices that require cooking in with jams and chutneys. A generous square of fabric can be gathered together around the ingredients and tied into a bag with natural string or twine. Alternatively, you can buy little drawstring muslin bags made specifically for this purpose.

SEALING Once poured into jars, hot jam should be sealed in some way. With mason jars, the seal forms part of the lid, but jars with ordinary lids require extra treatment. In Britain, we use waxed disks, which come in various sizes. In the United States, a layer of paraffin wax is preferred; this is readily available where canning supplies are sold. Be sure to follow the manufacturer's instructions for melting and pouring the paraffin.

LABELS Label all your preserves so you know how long they have been stored. Chutneys and pickles, which benefit from a maturing period, also need to be labeled with this information.

preserving techniques

There are two basic methods for making jam. The traditional method involves cooking the fruit before adding the sugar and boiling to setting point. The macerating method requires leaving the fruit and sugar, which have a lower sugar-to-fruit ratio, together, ideally overnight, to draw out the juices and intensify the flavors, before boiling to a set. This method gives a softer-setting jam with a more syrupy consistency.

JAM: THE TRADITIONAL METHOD

COOKING THE FRUIT   Place the fruit in a preserving pan with some water, the quantity of which will vary with the type of fruit. Bush fruits may not need any water, as they will quickly break up and release their juices when heated and mashed with a spoon. Harder fruits, however, will definitely need some water and a longer cooking time to soften them and release the pectin and acid. Simmer the fruits gently. Plums and blueberries should be cooked until their skins are soft. Once sugar is added, skins may become tough if they haven't been cooked enough before.

ADDING THE SUGAR   Use white granulated sugar. The amount of sugar needed varies, but the minimum amount recommended for 1 pound of bulky fruit (or about 3½ cups of bush fruits) is 1⅓ cups. Ideally, use 1½–1¾ cups for a softer-set jam and 2 cups for a traditionally prepared jam. With experience you'll discover the effect you prefer.

It is best to warm the sugar in a bowl in the oven (about 20 minutes on its lowest setting) before adding it to the fruit, as this will help it to dissolve quicker. Take the jam off the heat and allow it to cool slightly so it isn't still boiling when the sugar is added. Stir continuously over low heat until the sugar has completely dissolved. (If the jam comes to the boil before the sugar has completely dissolved, it may crystallize during storage.)

BOILING THE JAM   When the sugar has dissolved, turn up the heat and bring the jam to the boil. How long it needs to boil will vary, and this is something that becomes more apparent with experience. The jam needs to maintain a high temperature to reduce and thicken so it will set as it cools. Sometimes this can take a matter of minutes and on other occasions up to half an hour, depending on how much water the jam contains. This stage is often referred to as a rolling boil.

TESTING FOR SETTING POINT   After 5–10 minutes of rapid boiling, test the jam to see if it has reached setting point. This can be done in several ways (see below). Remove the pan from the heat while testing, so the jam doesn't overcook.

The cold plate test   Put a small plate in the freezer to chill beforehand. Drip a pool of jam onto the plate with a spoon and allow it to cool for a few seconds, then draw your finger through the jam. If setting point has been reached, the surface will wrinkle. When you raise your finger from the plate, the jam will form a strand, rather than dripping off.

Using a jam thermometer
Dip the thermometer into hot water, then push it into the jam, preferably in the center of the pan. If the temperature reaches 220°F, setting point has been reached.

The flake test   Dip a wooden spoon into the jam, then hold it above the pan. Leave it to cool for a few seconds, then let the jam fall off the spoon back into the pan. If the jam has a sticky consistency and forms strands or flakes that hang onto the spoon, setting point has been reached.

If setting point has not been reached, place the pan back on the heat and continue to boil rapidly, testing again at 5-minute intervals.

SKIMMING During boiling, a scum sometimes forms on jam, jelly, or marmalade due to bubbles rising to the surface. This scum is harmless but can spoil the appearance of the preserve. Stir in a small knob of butter to help disperse the scum or use a metal spoon to scoop it away.

DISPERSING THE FRUIT Whole fruits or large pieces of fruit often rise up to the top of a jam, and as the jam sets, they are likely to stay put. If you are making a softer-set jam with pieces in, you may have to live with this, but for a thicker set, leave the jam for 5–10 minutes prior to placing in jars, then stir to distribute the pieces evenly.

FILLING AND STORING Have your hot jars and jar funnel ready. Pour the jam into the jars, leaving ¼ inch between the top of the jam and the rim, if using a mason jar, or ½ inch if sealing with paraffin wax and ordinary lids (see page 9). Apply paraffin, if using, right away. If using mason jars or other canning jars, follow manufacturer's instructions for covering and sealing. Store the jam, once cool, in a dry, cool cabinet or pantry.

JAM: THE MACERATING METHOD

Allowing fruit and sugar to macerate together before cooking draws the moisture and juices from the fruit and preserves the flavor. Cooking times are reduced and flavors intensified, and it is possible to use a lower sugar content (see page 7), depending on the sweetness of the fruit.

Prepare the fruit as directed and place in a ceramic, glass, or stainless steel bowl. Add the sugar, cover with a plate, or push a piece of waxed paper down onto the surface of the fruit to hold in the moisture, and leave to macerate: softer fruits for 6–8 hours and harder fruits

for up to 36 hours. You will see the sugar soak up the juices and a considerable amount of liquid begin to dissolve the sugar.

Pour the fruit into a preserving pan and stir over a gentle heat until the sugar has completely dissolved. Occasionally, the mixture is left to macerate again, but if not, bring the jam to setting point as for the traditional method and pour into the jars.

MAKING MARMALADE

If making citrus marmalade, it is important to cook the citrus rind properly, and this can take 1½–3 hours, depending on the method you choose. Poaching the oranges whole is my preferred method, but removing the rind and shredding it at the outset is an alternative. If you use waxed fruits, you will need to scrub them before use, but just a rinse will do for unwaxed ones.

POACHING Wash the whole fruits and place in a heavy, lidded casserole with a tight-fitting lid. Pour in enough water to just cover the fruits, so they begin to float, then cover and place in a preheated oven, 350°F, to poach for 2½–3 hours, by which time the skins will be softened. Leave until cool enough to handle, then, using a slotted spoon, lift the fruits from the liquid, halve them, and scoop out the insides, gathering together all the pith and seeds and collecting any juice. Slice the rind into strips. Place the seeds and pith in a square of muslin, and tie into a bundle with string. Pour any collected juice back in with the cooking liquid.

PARING THE RIND FIRST Cut the uncooked fruits in half and squeeze out and collect the juice. Save the seeds. Pare the rind and chop into thin shreds. Chop the pith finely. Place the seeds in a square of muslin and tie into a bundle with string. Place everything in a pan and add enough water to cover, then leave overnight to soak. The next day, bring to the boil, then simmer for about 1½ hours until the rind is softened and cooked through. Remove the bundle of seeds.

From now on, the method is the same whichever form of preparation you used. Add warmed sugar and stir to dissolve, then complete in the same way as if making jam. Once setting point is reached, leave the marmalade for 10–15 minutes, then remove the muslin bag (if using the poaching method) and stir to distribute the rind shreds before pouring into jars.

MAKING JELLIES

A jelly is similar to a jam but does not contain pieces of fruit. The fruit is cooked with water, then poured into a jelly bag and allowed to drip through. Only the juice is used. Fruits most suited to jelly making generally have a high pectin content (see page 7).

When making jellies, cook the fruit first with water until tender. You can mash the fruit with a spoon at this stage before pouring it into a jelly bag suspended over a container to catch the drips. For the clearest jelly, allow plenty of time for the juice to drip through (overnight is ideal), and don't squeeze the bag, as this will make the jelly cloudy. (It is often possible to reboil the contents of the jelly bag using half the original amount of water and pour it through the bag again to get the maximum amount of juice and pectin from the fruit.)

Now measure the juice to work out how much sugar will be needed. The general rule is ¾ cup sugar to every 1 cup juice, which will make roughly 1lb 10oz jelly. Place the juice in a preserving pan and add warmed sugar as for jam-making, stirring until completely dissolved. Bring to a rapid boil and cook on a high heat to reach settting point, as before.

Rather than waste the residue in the jelly bag, push it through a food mill, collect the purée, and sweeten it, to use for pie fillings.

MAKING CURDS

Fruit curds have shorter keeping times than jams and jellies—2 months unopened in a cool place. Make them in small jars, for once opened, they should be kept in the refrigerator and eaten within 2 weeks. You can also pour curds into suitable containers and freeze them for 6 months.

Curds are made using sugar, butter, and eggs and so are more like a custard than a jam. They are best suited to tart, fruity flavors. So that the eggs don't

curdle or cook on too high a heat, it is best to use a double boiler or a basin set over a pan of simmering water. You will have to stir the curd continuously for 20–30 minutes until it thickens and will coat the back of the spoon, but the result will be well worth the effort.

Prepare a fruit purée first by cooking the fruit in the minimum amount of water, if any at all, until tender. Softer fruits, such as raspberries and blueberries, require hardly any cooking, while gooseberries and squash need more. Press the fruit through the fine disk of a food mill or a sieve and collect the purée.

MAKING CHUTNEYS AND PICKLES

Chutneys are made from fruits and vegetables mixed with vinegar, sugar, and spices. They are easy to make, generally just requiring all the ingredients to be thrown together in a preserving pan and cooked for a couple of hours. It is important to pack in jars with vinegar-proof lids.

Try to leave chutneys and pickles to mature for 6–8 weeks, or even a few months, before eating, as the flavors mellow over time.

Pickles and chutneys both require vinegars flavored with spices, and all the recipes in this book give instructions for making these from scratch. However, you can also make your own vinegars using the recipes that follow—two for pickling vinegars and two for sweetened pickling vinegars, which are suitable for pickling fruits and fruit chutneys.

PICKLING VINEGAR

To 1 quart cider, malt, or wine vinegar, add:
piece of fresh gingerroot approx. ¾ x 2½ inches, peeled and finely sliced
1 tbsp each black peppercorns, mustard seeds, celery seeds
8 dried red chilies
2 tsp each whole allspice, whole cloves, whole coriander seeds

Mix all the spices together and divide between clean, sterlilized bottles. Fill the bottles with the vinegar and seal with corks or stoppers. Leave the vinegar to infuse for 6–8 weeks, giving the bottles an occasional shake. Strain out the spices from the vinegar before using.

For a quicker version:

Place all the ingredients in a bowl and place this over a pan of simmering water, or use a double boiler. Allow the vinegar to warm through without boiling, then remove it from the heat and leave the spices to steep in the warm vinegar for 2–3 hours. Strain out the spices from the vinegar before using.

SWEET PICKLING VINEGAR

To 1 quart cider, malt, or wine vinegar, add:
1 cinnamon stick
1 tbsp each whole allspice, whole coriander seeds, whole cloves, white peppercorns
5 blades of mace
2 dried red chilies (optional)
3½ cups brown or white sugar

Mix the spices together and divide between clean bottles. Warm the vinegar and dissolve the sugar in it, then fill the bottles with the vinegar and seal with corks or stoppers. Leave to infuse for 6–8 weeks, giving the bottles an occasional shake. Strain out the spices from the vinegar before using.

For a quicker version:

Place 2½ cups white wine vinegar, a rounded ¾ cup of sugar, a ¾-inch square piece of fresh gingerroot, and a few whole allspice berries and black peppercorns in a pan, and stir over a low heat to dissolve the sugar. Turn up the heat and boil for 1 minute, then remove from the heat. Strain the spices from the vinegar before using.

MAKING NECTARS AND SYRUPS

Nectars and syrups make good use of fruit that is overripe and not suitable for jam-making; they are also easy to make. Bush fruits, such as blackberries, loganberries, and raspberries, are suitable, as are citrus fruits and foraged ingredients, such as rose hips, elderflowers, and elderberries.

For all bush fruits the method is the same. Put the fruit in a bowl and break it up with a spoon, then add only a minimal amount of water, if any at all. Place the bowl over a pan of simmering water and heat through to extract all the juice from the fruit. Pour the fruit through a jelly bag and collect the juice underneath, leaving it to drip overnight.

Add a scant 1½ cups sugar to every 2 cups juice and stir together over a low heat until dissolved; do not allow it to boil. Strain into clean bottles, filling to within 1 inch of the top of the bottle. Cork securely or use bottles with ceramic stoppers and wires. The bottles will now need to be sterilized so that the contents keep for a long time. (Alternatively—and this is the easier option—the syrup or nectar can be poured into suitable containers and frozen.)

To sterilize, place some folded newspaper or a trivet in the bottom of a pan and place the bottles on top. Add cold water almost to the top of the bottles, then bring to the boil and simmer for 20 minutes. Make sure that the bottles are securely sealed, then store them in a cool, dry place.

KEEPING TIMES

The jams and jellies will keep, unopened, in a cool, dark place for at least 6 months, and the other preserves will keep for 6–12 months. Keeping times will vary once jars and bottles are opened, but you'll find that these preserves are so delicious that they will be eaten up long before there is any chance of their deteriorating.

PROBLEM SOLVING

Why jam goes moldy

Mold is most often caused by a failure to seal the jam adequately while it is still very hot. Alternatively, jars may have been damp or cold when used, weren't filled right to the top, or have been stored in a damp place. Other possible causes are insufficient evaporation of water during the preliminary cooking and/or too short a period of boiling after the sugar has been added. Jam with a good set is less likely to go moldy, while a softer-set jam will be more inclined to spoil. Sometimes mold can form because the fruit was picked on a wet day. Mold is not harmful to the jam but it may affect the taste slightly. If it is removed, the jam can be boiled up again and re-packed in clean, sterilized jars.

Why tiny bubbles appear

Bubbles indicate fermentation, which is usually the result of too little sugar in relation to the quantity of fruit. When jam is not reduced sufficiently, this can also affect the proportion of sugar.

Why fruit rises in the jam

When the fruit is in big pieces or is used whole, such as strawberries, the pieces tend to rise in the jam after it is poured. To keep them dispersed throughout the preserve, leave the jam in the pan for 10–15 minutes after setting point is reached to thicken slightly, then stir before pouring it into the jars. The syrupy consistency of softer-set jams means that fruit will invariably rise. The same problem may occur with rind in marmalade, and the solution of waiting and stirring is the same.

Why jam crystallizes

Too much sugar or too little acid is usually the cause. Low-acid fruits benefit from the addition of acid in the form of lemon juice. Making sure that the sugar has dissolved completely before bringing the jam to a fast boil also helps. Sometimes overripe fruit is responsible, or storing the jam in too warm a place.

Why jam won't set

Low levels of pectin, due to using fruits containing very little pectin or overripe fruit, may make it difficult to reach setting point. Other reasons include under-boiling the fruit, so that the pectin is not fully extracted, or insufficient evaporation of the water before the sugar is added, in which case return the jam to the preserving pan and boil it further. It is also possible to overcook jam after sugar has been added, for which there is no remedy. For fruits low in pectin, such as strawberries and cherries, you can add more pectin in the form of fruits (such as lemon juice, apples, or redcurrants).

Why jam shrinks in the jar

Shrinkage is caused by the jam being inadequately covered or sealed, or failure to store it in a cool, dark and dry place.

jams

Jam isn't just for spreading on bread— try it between the layers of a cake, or add a spoonful to some vanilla ice cream, or use it to jazz up some bland rice pudding. Basically, jam is just fruit and sugar cooked together to make the fruit keep. The fruit can be puréed or left in pieces to add texture. The result is one of life's sweet little extras.

Makes about 3¾ cups
4 pints blackberries
1 star anise
3 cloves
1 small cinnamon stick
juice of 2 lemons
3 cups warmed sugar (see page 10)

spiced blackberry jam

I don't often choose to spice up the fruits when jam making, preferring for the simple fruit flavors to dominate; however, here a mixed handful of warming spices suits this autumnal fruit preserve perfectly.

1 Place the blackberries in a saucepan with the star anise, cloves, cinnamon stick, and 2 tablespoons of water (just enough so the fruit doesn't catch on the pan). Bring them to simmering point and continue cooking until they are tender and juicy, mashing them with a spoon.

2 Remove the cinnamon stick and press the berries through the fine disk of a food mill or a sieve. If you prefer a chunkier-textured jam, there is no need to purée the fruit at all: simply fish out the spices with a spoon and continue with the whole blackberry pulp.

3 Add the lemon juice to the blackberries and place them in a preserving pan; heat through, stirring gently. Add the warmed sugar to the pan and stir until completely dissolved, then turn up the heat and boil the jam rapidly to reach setting point (see page 10). Skim if necessary (see page 11).

4 Pour the jam into hot, sterilized jars (see page 8) and seal (see page 11).

Makes about 4¾ cups
4 pints blackberries
1 star anise
3 cloves
1 small cinnamon stick

4 nectarines (approx. ½ pound when
    skinned and stoned)
juice of 2 lemons
4 cups warmed sugar (see page 10)

spiced blackberry & nectarine jam

I discovered this combination when I found a bargain pack of nectarines at the supermarket. They bring a welcome sharpness to the mellow flavor of blackberries as well as an appealing texture.

Cook and purée the blackberries and spices as in steps 1–2 on page 16. To skin the nectarines, place them in a bowl and pour boiling water over them. Leave for a few minutes, then drain off the water and replace with cold water; the skins should slip easily off the fruit. Cut the nectarines into quarters, removing the stones, then cut each quarter into thirds (smaller pieces if you like a finer-textured preserve). Place the blackberries, lemon juice, nectarines, and sugar in a preserving pan and cook as in step 3 on page 16. Leave the jam for 5 minutes, then stir to redistribute the nectarine pieces. Pack the jam as before.

Makes about 3¾ cups
2 pounds apricots
3 cups sugar
juice of 1 small lemon

apricot jam

This jam contains slightly less sugar than most, resulting in a softer set, and the apricots are left in big chunks. Because of this, it is inevitable that the fruit will rise to the top of the jar, rather than being suspended evenly throughout the jam. This doesn't matter—you can simply allocate an apricot half for every serving. One apricot piece will squash perfectly under the knife to fill a discuit, for example. The cooking time is kept to a minimum, so keeping the flavor at its utmost.

1 Skin the fruits by placing them in a bowl, pouring boiling water over them, and leaving them for a few minutes, then replacing the hot water with cold. The skins should then be easy to peel away. Keep the skins to one side. Halve the fruits and remove the stones. Place the skins and stones in a piece of muslin and tie it into a bag with string.

2 Place the sugar and lemon juice in a ceramic or glass bowl and add ¾ cup water; tuck the muslin bag in among the other ingredients. Push a piece of waxed paper down onto the surface to cover it and leave the bowl in the refrigerator overnight.

3 By the next day, the juice will have been drawn out of the fruits into the sugar, which will be partly dissolved. Pour the contents of the bowl into a preserving pan and heat gently, stirring all the time until the sugar has completely dissolved. Simmer gently for 10 minutes without stirring, so the apricot halves stay intact, then remove them from the syrup using a slotted spoon. Remove and discard the muslin bag.

4 Bring the syrup to the boil and boil rapidly to reach setting point (see page 10), then quickly put the apricots back into the syrup and bring to the boil again. Remove the jam from the heat. Skim if necessary (see page 11).

5 Spoon the apricots into hot, sterilized jars (see page 8), dividing them equally, then pour the syrup over them, filling the jars up to the top. Seal the jars (see page 11) and leave them to cool upside down.

Makes about 3¾ cups
1 vanilla bean
2 pounds apricots

3 cups sugar
juice of 1 small lemon

apricot & vanilla jam

This combination seems so French to me. With its softer, syrupy set, this preserve might be eaten as a dessert, perhaps with unsweetened whipped cream. Or enjoy it on a croissant with your coffee.

First slice the vanilla pod in half lengthwise and scrape out the seeds with the blade of a knife. Then follow the instructions for Apricot Jam, adding the seeds to the ingredients when placing them in a bowl and tucking the pod pieces in among the fruit, then leave the mixture to macerate overnight. Remove the pod pieces before filling and sealing the jars.

Makes about 3½ cups

3 pints white currants
4 red gooseberries (optional)
juice of 1 lemon
2 red chilies (or more if you wish),
    deseeded and minced
warmed sugar (see page 10; for quantity
    see step 3)

white currant & red chili jam

White currants are another fruit with a lovely tart flavor, which makes them just perfect for jam making. This jam, with its additional chili kick, is subtle enough to eat on sourdough toast for breakfast but could also be taken up a notch, by adding more chili to taste, and serving as a relish to go with cheese. And if you have a few red gooseberries to add to the currants, they'll give this jam a beautiful rose hue.

1 Strip the white currants from their stalks by running the tines of a fork over their stems. Place the currants and gooseberries, if using, in a pan along with the lemon juice and ⅝ cup water. Simmer until the fruits are soft and bursting.

2 Push the fruit through the fine disk of a food mill, or a sieve, collecting the resulting purée in a measuring pitcher.

3 Allow ¾ cup sugar to every 1 cup purée.

4 Gently heat the purée and add the minced chilies, then the warmed sugar. Stir the jam over a low heat until the sugar has completely dissolved. Turn up the heat and boil rapidly to reach setting point (see page 10). Skim if necessary (see page 11).

5 Pour the jam into hot, sterilized jars (see page 8) and seal (see page 11).

Makes about 4 cups
4 pints raspberries
juice of 1 small lemon
3 cups warmed sugar (see page 10)

raspberry jam

Some people like jam with lots of seeds in it; some don't. With raspberry jam you have a choice. If you love the flavor of this fruit but find the seeds annoying, push the softened fruit through a sieve for a smoother finish. The result will taste just as good as the kind with the seeds in it.

1 Place the raspberries and lemon juice in a preserving pan. Heat them gently to draw out the juice, mashing the berries with a spoon until the fruit is soft and there is plenty of juice. If you want a smooth jam, push the fruit through a sieve to remove the seeds.

2 Add the warmed sugar to the fruit and stir over a gentle heat until the sugar has completely dissolved. Turn up the heat and bring the jam to a fast boil until it reaches setting point (see page 10). Skim if necessary (see page 11).

3 Pour the jam into hot, sterilized jars (see page 8) and seal (see page 11).

Makes about 5 cups
1 pint gooseberries, stems and blossom
  ends removed
2 pints strawberries, hulled
4 cups warmed sugar (see page 10)
juice of 1 lemon

strawberry & gooseberry jam

Gooseberries and strawberries make a good partnership as the higher pectin levels found in gooseberries offset the lower levels in the strawberries. I also like a jam that not only tastes great but is colorful too; this one wins on both counts.

1 Place the gooseberries in a preserving pan with 3 tablespoons of water. Heat gently and simmer until the berries are just soft, then add the strawberries. Cook for 5 minutes until the fruits begin to lose their shape and the juice starts to run.

2 Add the warmed sugar and the lemon juice to the fruit. Stir gently over a low heat until the sugar has completely dissolved. Turn up the heat and boil rapidly to reach setting point (see page 10). Skim if necessary (see page 11).

3 Pour the jam into hot, sterilized jars (see page 8) and seal (see page 11).

Makes about 4 cups

1 vanilla bean

4 pints strawberries, hulled; larger fruits
    halved

3 scant cups sugar

juice of 3 small lemons

strawberry & vanilla jam

Let's face it, strawberry jam is the real classic. This fragile fruit isn't a great keeper, so for the best jam, capture the fruit at its freshest, preserving it in recognizable chunks. This really is summer in a jar. Here I have teamed strawberries with vanilla, the perfect partner, which as far as I'm concerned you can't ever get enough of.

This recipe uses slightly less sugar than a traditional strawberry jam might and consequently has a softer set, which means if you are feeling really gluttonous, you can eat it straight from the jar. Or swirl a few spoonfuls through a mixture of mascarpone and plain yogurt for a fast dessert. Or dollop it onto a freshly baked biscuit—eating it quickly before the jam oozes away over the sides.

1 Split the vanilla bean lengthwise into four pieces and place in a bowl with the strawberries, tucking the bean pieces in among the fruit. Cover with the sugar and leave for 12 hours or overnight.

2 Pour the fruit, vanilla bean, and juice into a preserving pan and add the lemon juice. Cook over a low heat until the sugar has dissolved, stirring only now and then so that the fruit stays intact. Turn up the heat and boil rapidly to reach setting point (see page 10). Skim if necessary (see page 11).

3 Remove the vanilla bean pieces, scrape the seeds out of them, and add these to the jam, disposing of the beans. Stir the seeds through the jam.

4 Pour the jam into hot, sterilized jars (see page 8) and seal (see page 11).

Makes about 2½ cups
1 pound plums, halved and stoned
2 cups warmed sugar (see page 10)

plum jam

Where I live, we have our own, locally grown plum variety, the Blaisdon Red plum, so naturally that is my particular favorite for this jam. Most years, come late summer, the trees are dripping with them, so there is always lots of jam making to be done. Of course, other plum varieties will do just as well.

1 Place the plums in a pan with ½ cup water and bring to a simmer, then cook gently for 10 minutes until the plums are soft but still intact.

2 Add the warmed sugar to the fruit and stir over a low heat until all the sugar has dissolved, then turn up the heat and boil rapidly to reach setting point (see page 10). Skim if necessary (see page 11).

3 Pour the jam into hot, sterilized jars (see page 8) and seal (see page 11).

damson jam

Damsons make superb jam, one of the best. It is an old-fashioned fruit, which isn't so often used commercially for preserving. The bold and traditional character of this fruit makes it ideal as a single-fruit jam.

Follow the recipe for Plum Jam, using damsons, but do not attempt to remove the stones before cooking. Spoon off any stones that float to the surface, then leave the cooked fruit to cool before using your hands to find and remove the rest. Once you are sure you have removed all the stones, add the sugar and bring to setting point as before.

Makes about 5 cups
1 pound plums, halved and stoned

1 pound marrow squash flesh,
 cut into chunks
4 cups sugar

plum & marrow squash jam

A great jam to help make just a few plums go a long way. Marrow squash acts as a chameleon here, bulking out the jam and soaking up the fruity sweetness of the plums.

Put the plums and marrow squash together in a pan with ½ cup water and continue as for Plum Jam.

Makes about 5 cups
3 pints raspberries
1½ pounds ripe peaches (5 or 6)
4¼ cups sugar
juice of 2 lemons

peach & raspberry jam

This jam is not only wonderfully fragrant but also gloriously colorful, with deep red raspberries dotted through with peach pieces. Here, as usual, I would opt for a chunky texture to set this preserve apart from anything you will ever find in a store. You can, of course, chop the peaches finer if you prefer.

1 Place the raspberries in a pan. Warm them gently to soften them and release their juice, mashing them with the back of a spoon.

2 When they are soft and juicy, push them through the fine disk of a food mill, or a sieve.

3 Place the raspberry purée, half of the sugar, and half of the lemon juice in a pan and bring to a simmer, then remove from the heat and pour into a ceramic or glass bowl. Cover the surface with waxed paper, pushed down onto the fruit, and leave the bowl in the fridge overnight.

4 Meanwhile, to skin the peaches, place them in a bowl and pour boiling water over them. Leave to steep for a few minutes, then pour off the water and replace with cold water; the skins should now easily peel away from the flesh. Cut the peaches into quarters and remove the stones, then cut each quarter in half, so the pieces are still quite chunky.

5 Place the peaches, remaining sugar, and lemon juice in a pan, bring just to simmering point, then remove from the heat. Pour the fruit into a glass or ceramic bowl and cover it with waxed paper as described for the raspberries; leave in the fridge overnight.

6 The next day, combine the raspberries and peaches in a preserving pan and heat gently, stirring all the time to be sure that the sugar has completely dissolved. Turn up the heat and boil rapidly until setting point is reached (see page 10). Skim if necessary (see page 11). Leave for 5 minutes, then stir to distribute the peach pieces. Pour the jam into hot, sterilized jars (see page 8) and seal (see page 11).

Makes about 3 cups
2 pints cherries
1 generous cup warmed sugar (see page 10)
1 tbsp lemon juice

cherry jam

You can use a black cooking cherry, such as a Morello cherry, for this jam, or a paler dessert cherry, and the color of your jam will vary accordingly. If you grow your own, make sure to pick them as soon as they ripen, or the birds will eat all of them before you get the chance.

1 Pit the cherries, using a cherry stoner over a basin to catch any juice. Place the stones in a piece of muslin and tie it into a bag with string. Put the fruit and juice into a pan with 2 tablespoons water and simmer gently until the fruit is just cooked.

2 Add the warmed sugar and the lemon juice to the fruit and stir over a low heat until all the sugar has dissolved, then turn up the heat and boil rapidly to reach setting point (see page 10). Remove the muslin bag and leave the jam for 5–10 minutes, then stir to redistribute the cherries. Skim if necessary (see page 11).

3 Pour the jam into hot, sterilized jars (see page 8) and seal (see page 11).

Makes about 8 cups

2¼ cups rose hips
2¼ cups hawthorn hips ("haws")
2 cups rowan berries (optional)
2 cups sloes
1 pound crab apples or tart cooking
  apples, chopped
2 pints blackberries
1½ pints elderberries
⅞ cup hazelnuts, shelled and chopped
warmed sugar (see page 10; for quantity
  see step 3)

countryside jam

Foraging is such a satisfying pursuit—gathering food for free that has required no effort whatsoever to cultivate. In England, where I live, the hedgerows yield many edible fruits in the fall, and I've used some of these in this jam, along with fruits that can be found in any good supermarket. American readers may not find rowan (European mountain ash) growing wild, but any region containing woodland or agricultural land will yield useful ingredients. In any case, you'll need to take a flexible approach, since not all of your chosen fruits will be ripe at the same time. Of course, not all berries are edible, so if you don't know how to recognize the ones that are, this jam isn't for you. Countryside Jam is autumn in a jar.

1 Pick over the fruit and remove the stalks. Place the hips, haws, rowan berries, if using, sloes, and apples in a pan with just enough water to cover the fruit, so it begins to float. Simmer for approximately 15 minutes until the fruit is soft and the apples fluffy.

2 Push the fruit mixture through the fine disk of a food mill or a sieve and collect the puréed pulp in a preserving pan. Add the blackberries, elderberries, and nuts and simmer for 15 minutes.

3 Measure the cooked fruit and add an equal amount of warmed sugar. Stir over a low heat until all the sugar has dissolved, then turn up the heat and boil rapidly to reach setting point (see page 10). Skim if necessary (see page 11).

4 Pour the jam into hot, sterilized jars (see page 8) and seal (see page 11).

Makes about 4 cups
2 pounds pears, peeled, cored, and cut
   into chunky slices
juice of 1 large lemon
3 cups sugar
1 vanilla bean

pear & vanilla jam

This jam is another of my particular favorites and is one I find it hard to live without. The specks of real vanilla dotted throughout the pale jam show its quality, infusing their aromatic flavor. Here, macerating the pears also brings out the most flavor from the fruit.

1 Place the pears in a bowl with the lemon juice to stop them from discoloring. Sprinkle the sugar over the fruit and add ¾ cup water.

2 Slice the vanilla bean in half lengthwise and scrape out the seeds, then tuck the bean in among the pears and add the seeds. Cover the bowl with a plate and leave overnight for the sugar to soak up some of the juices from the fruit.

3 The next day, pour the contents of the bowl into a preserving pan and stir over a low heat until the sugar has dissolved, then turn up the heat and boil rapidly to reach setting point (see page 10), by which time the pear pieces will be translucent. Skim if necessary (see page 11).

4 Remove the vanilla bean, then pour the jam into hot, sterilized jars (see page 8) and seal (see page 11).

pear & chocolate jam

After traveling in France, my neighbors brought me back some pear jam, which had tiny nuggets of chocolate suspended through the syrup. This is my interpretation of that unusual preserve.

You will need 2 cups coarsely grated good-quality dark chocolate. Make the Pear & Vanilla Jam and spoon it into the jars in layers, interspersed with sprinkled grated chocolate. The chocolate will melt on contact with the hot jam, but the aim is to have chocolate speckled throughout, rather than mixed in, so that the overall colour of the jam is pale.

Makes about 6 cups
2 pounds pumpkin or butternut squash
  flesh
1 vanilla bean
4¾ cups sugar
juice of 2 lemons

pumpkin & vanilla jam

This recipe is a great one to make, as an alternative to pumpkin pie, when you are faced with a pile of scooped-out pumpkin innards after making jack-o'-lanterns. The natural sweetness of the pumpkin flesh is just perfect for making into jam.

1 Place the pumpkin in a pan with just enough water to stop it from catching, and cook over a moderate heat for 10–15 minutes until it is cooked through but still retains its shape. Drain off any excess juices, and when the pumpkin is cool enough to handle, chop it into finer pieces.

2 Slice the vanilla bean in half lengthwise and scrape out the seeds with the blade of a knife. Place the pumpkin, sugar, and lemon juice in a bowl, tuck the vanilla bean pieces in among the pumpkin, and add the seeds. Cover with a piece of waxed paper pushed down onto the surface and leave overnight.

3 The next day, pour the contents of the bowl into a preserving pan and stir over a low heat until all the sugar has dissolved, then turn up the heat and boil rapidly to reach setting point (see page 10). Skim if necessary (see page 11).

4 Pour the jam into hot, sterilized jars (see page 8) and seal (see page 11).

Makes about 4 cups
1 pound apricots
4 stalks (approx. 1 pound) rhubarb, cut into
    short lengths
3 cups sugar
juice of 1 lemon

rhubarb & apricot jam

This jam is an absolute star. Everyone who has tasted it has been knocked out by how full of flavor it is and the perfection of this combination of fruits. The pinkness of the rhubarb pieces, along with the chunky apricot halves, also makes it a real treat visually. If you make only one jam in this book (hopefully you'll make more than that!), this is the one.

1 Skin the apricots by placing them in a bowl and pouring boiling water over them. Leave for a few minutes, then drain the water and replace with cold water. The skins should then be easy to peel away with a knife. Cut into halves and remove the stones.

2 Place all the ingredients in a bowl, cover with a plate, and leave for 1 hour.

3 Pour the contents of the bowl into a preserving pan and stir over a low heat to dissolve the sugar. Turn up the heat and bring just to simmering point, then remove from the heat. Pour everything into a glass or ceramic bowl, cover with a piece of waxed paper pushed down onto the surface, and refrigerate overnight.

4 The next day, pour the contents of the bowl back into the preserving pan and stir over a low heat until all the sugar has dissolved, then turn up the heat and boil rapidly to reach setting point (see page 10). Skim if necessary (see page 11).

5 Pour the jam into hot, sterilized jars (see page 8) and seal (see page 11).

Makes about 4½ cups
8 stalks (approx. 2¼ pounds) rhubarb, cut
  into short lengths

finely grated zest and juice of 3 limes
3¾ cups sugar

rhubarb & lime jam

Rhubarb is often teamed up with orange, but I much prefer to combine it with lime instead.
This is a medley made in heaven.

Place all the ingredients in a bowl, cover with a plate and leave for 1 hour.
Then follow steps 3–5 of Rhubarb & Apricot Jam.

Makes about 2½ cups
1 pound figs, stalks removed and chopped into small pieces

2 cups warmed sugar (see page 10)
juice of 1 lemon

green fig jam

Green or purple figs are suitable for jam making. Figs do not ripen any further once picked from the tree, and they don't have much flavor when unripe, so pick or buy them already ripe enough to use. This jam has a beautiful rich color and is dotted throughout with seeds.

1 Place the figs in a pan with 2 tablespoons water, heat gently to a simmer, and cook until soft and juicy.

2 Add the warmed sugar and the lemon juice to the fruit and stir over low heat until all the sugar has dissolved, then turn up the heat and boil rapidly to reach setting point (see page 10). Leave for 10 minutes, then stir to distribute the fig pieces throughout the jam. Skim if necessary (see page 11).

3 Pour the jam into hot, sterilized jars (see page 8) and seal (see page 11).

Makes about 4½ cups
1¼ pounds figs
1 pound pears, peeled, cored, and diced
finely grated zest and juice of 1 large orange
   and 1 small lemon

3¾ cups sugar
8 green cardamom pods, crushed
   and pods discarded

fig & pear jam

Both main ingredients here are low in pectin, so definitely need help from the lemon and orange additions to boost their setting power. Green cardamom seeds add a unique and unusual twist.

Prepare the figs as above, then place all ingredients in a bowl and leave for 1 hour. Pour into a preserving pan, stir over a low heat to dissolve the sugar, then turn up the heat and bring to simmering point. Pour into a glass or ceramic bowl, cover with waxed paper pushed down onto the surface, and refrigerate overnight. Next day, pour the contents back into the pan and stir over a low heat, then turn up the heat and boil rapidly to reach setting point (see page 10). Pack as above.

Makes about 2 cups
juice and finely pared zest of 1 small lemon
1 pound green tomatoes, finely chopped
1⅝ cups sugar
2 pieces of stem ginger, about 1 inch in
    diameter, finely sliced

green tomato jam

Usually thought of as an ingredient for chutney, green tomatoes were once popular for jam making but have somehow fallen from favor. This recipe will prove that a fashion revival is due. The lemon peel and stem ginger work well here to produce a candied jam with a fabulous color.

1 Place the lemon zest in a pan with just enough water to cover it and simmer for about 1 hour until soft. Drain the zest, discarding the liquid.

2 Place the tomatoes and lemon juice in a bowl with the sugar and leave overnight for the sugar to soak up some of the juices from the fruit.

3 Next day, pour the contents of the bowl into a preserving pan and add the zest. Stir over a low heat until the sugar has dissolved, then turn up the heat and boil rapidly to reach setting point (see page 10). Skim if necessary (see page 11).

4 Stir in the stem ginger, then pour the jam into hot, sterilized jars (see page 8) and seal (see page 11).

green tomato & angelica jam

I came across this combination in *Tomatoes and How to Grow Them* by F. R. Castle, dated 1938. Angelica is an interesting herb to grow and makes a towering plant, showy enough to work in the perennial border. If you don't have fresh angelica, you may be able to buy candied stems.

Use 2 or 3 fresh stems, about 5 inches tall, or a scant ¼ cup candied pieces, and follow the recipe for Green Tomato Jam, omitting the stem ginger. If using fresh angelica, choose young stems. Pour boiling water over them and allow to steep for 5 minutes, then drain and shred finely. Add to the tomatoes at the beginning. If using candied stems, chop them finely and add at the end of the recipe instead of the stem ginger.

Makes about 5¼ cups
1½ cups black currants
1½ cups red currants
2 cups strawberries
2 cups raspberries
4¼ cups warmed sugar (see page 10)

tutti frutti jam

Mixed-fruit jams are a good way of using up small amounts of fruits. If you can't find black currants (not to be confused with small raisins), use all red ones. Combining fruits with high pectin levels and those with low levels (see page 7) is a good way to help the jam to set.

1 Strip the black and red currants from their stalks by running the tines of a fork over the stems. Place the currants in a preserving pan with enough water just to stop the fruits from catching on the bottom of the pan. Bring to the boil, then simmer for 15–20 minutes.

2 Add the strawberries and raspberries and simmer for another 10 minutes. Add the warmed sugar to the fruit and stir over a low heat until all the sugar has dissolved. Turn up the heat and boil rapidly to reach setting point (see page 10). Skim if necessary (see page 11).

3 Pour the jam into hot, sterilized jars (see page 8) and seal (see page 11).

Makes about 3¾ cups
2 pints gooseberries, stems and blossom
   ends removed

3 rounded cups sugar
juice of 2 small lemons

gooseberry jam

Gooseberries make a sharp jam that works equally well as a sweet or savory accompaniment. The first varieties, ready to pick in early summer, herald the beginning of a season of luscious fruits, and their tartness makes them ideal for jam making. Later varieties get sweeter and can be eaten raw.

1 Place all the ingredients in a preserving pan and heat gently until simmering. Remove immediately from the heat and pour the contents into a ceramic or glass bowl. Cover the surface with waxed paper, pushing it down onto the fruit. Leave the bowl overnight in the refrigerator.

2 The next day, pour the contents of the bowl back into the preserving pan and heat gently, stirring to be sure that all the sugar has dissolved. Then turn up the heat and boil rapidly to reach setting point (see page 10). This takes very little time to achieve—only 5–10 minutes—and you need to watch that the syrup doesn't burn. Skim if necessary (see page 11).

3 Pour the jam into hot, sterilized jars (see page 8) and seal (see page 11).

Makes about 3¾ cups
handful of fresh elderflowers
2 pints gooseberries, stems and blossom
   ends removed

3 rounded cups sugar
juice of 2 small lemons

gooseberry & elderflower jam

How convenient that elderflowers are in season at the same time as early gooseberries. Here, again, elderflowers bring their unique and delicate flavor to a classic British combination.

First, shake the flowers, face down, to remove any unwanted creatures, then wrap them in a piece of muslin and tie into a bundle. Follow the recipe for Gooseberry Jam, pushing the elderflower bundle in among the gooseberries during their initial simmer and when being left to macerate overnight. Remove the bundle before returning the fruit to the preserving pan for the final cooking time.

Makes about 4 cups
1 pound peaches, quartered
   and stoned
1 pound pears, quartered
juice of 1 lemon
3⅓ cups sugar

peach & pear jam

This is another beautiful combination of delicate flavors. Here I have used a food mill to process the fruits, as I like the texture this method gives to the jam, and it cuts down on the initial preparation. You can, however, leave the fruits in whole chunks if you prefer, in which case you will need to peel and core the pears and skin and stone the peaches first.

1 Place the fruit in a pan with the lemon juice plus 1 tablespoon water and heat gently to release the juices and soften the fruit. Simmer for 10 minutes, then remove from the heat and leave to cool.

2 Press the fruit mixture through the fine disk of a food mill or a sieve and collect the puréed pulp in a preserving pan. Add the sugar to the fruit and stir over low heat until all the sugar has dissolved, then turn up the heat and boil rapidly to reach setting point (see page 10). Skim if necessary (see page 11).

3 Pour the jam into hot, sterilized jars (see page 8) and seal (see page 11).

Makes about 6 cups
1 pound cooking apples,
    roughly chopped
1 pound pears, roughly chopped
1 pound plums, halved
1¼ cups water
grated zest and juice of 1 small lemon
piece of gingerroot,
    approx. ¾ x 2½ inches, bruised
2 cloves
5 cups sugar

dumpsideary jam

Dumpsideary jam comes with an endearing name that smacks of tradition and uses a sumptuous medley of orchard fruits—apples, pears, and plums—that are in season together. Lightly spiced with ginger and cloves, it is sometimes known as High Dumpsideary while a similar jam without the spices is called mixty maxty. When you give a jar of this jam to someone, the name alone is sure to be a talking point.

1 Place all the fruits and the plum stones in a preserving pan along with 1¼ cups water and simmer gently until soft.

2 Remove the plum stones, then press all the fruit through the fine disk of a food mill or a sieve.

3 Place the resulting fruit purée in a preserving pan and add the lemon zest and juice. Tie the spices in a piece of muslin and add this to the pan along with the sugar. Heat the mixture slowly, stirring until the sugar has completely dissolved. Turn up the heat and boil rapidly to reach setting point (see page 10). Skim if necessary (see page 11).

4 Remove the spices. Pour the jam pour into hot, sterilized jars (see page 8) and seal (see page 11).

jellies

Made from the juices extracted from the fruit, jellies have a clarity and purity that is very attractive. The amber hues of crab apple, the glorious ruby shades of raspberry and red currant and the dense blackness of blackberry jellies are irresistible; when you hold the jar up to the light, it is like gazing through stained glass.

For quantity, see page 12
2 pounds black currants
juice of 1 small lemon (optional)
warmed sugar (see page 10; for quantity
   see step 5)

black currant jelly

This jelly is deep black and glassy, with a perfectly balanced rich, yet tart, flavor. Black currants (*Ribes nigrum*) have an unmistakable and robust taste, which makes them ideal for jams and jellies. Long enjoyed in Europe, they are gradually becoming more popular in the United States, but you may have trouble finding them. You might consider growing your own (check that your state permits this; for many years they were banned in some states for ecological reasons).

1 Strip the black currants from their stalks by running the tines of a fork through their stems.

2 Place the currants in a preserving pan with the lemon juice, if using, and 2⅓ cups water and simmer for 5 minutes until the currants start to burst and the juice flows. Remove from the heat and squash the currants with a fork.

3 Pour the currants and liquid into a jelly bag suspended over a bowl and leave it to drip for several hours or overnight (resisting the urge to help things along by squeezing the bag).

4 Since black currants have a high pectin content (see page 7), you can then increase the yield by tipping the pulp back into the preserving pan, along with 1¼ cups water, and boiling it for 5 minutes. Pour the pulp back into the jelly bag and leave it to drain for a few hours to extract the juice, collecting it in a pitcher.

5 Allow ¾ cup sugar for every cupful juice.

6 Heat the juice in a preserving pan over a low heat, then add the warmed sugar. Stir until the sugar has dissolved, then turn up the heat and boil rapidly until setting point is reached (see page 10). Skim if necessary (see page 11). Pour into hot, sterilized jars (see page 8) and seal (see page 11).

red currant & gooseberry jelly

Gooseberries are almost top of the list for pectin content with red currants not too far behind, so you can expect this jelly to have a good set. The red currants help to give this jelly a good color, which the gooseberries alone don't have.

Follow the recipe for Black Currant Jelly, but use 2½ cups each of red currants and gooseberries and 1½ cups water. Boil the currants and berries together until soft and bursting, then pour into a jelly bag and collect the juice in a pitcher. Don't boil the fruit pulp for a second time. Complete the jelly as before.

For quantity, see page 12
4 cups rose hips, stalks removed
2 pounds cooking or tart apples, roughly
   chopped
warmed sugar (see page 10; for quantity
   see step 2)

rose hip jelly

Perhaps surprisingly, the juice from these wild berries is rich in vitamin C and has a fantastic flavor. Since these fruits are stuffed full of tiny seeds and short itching hairs that are completely inedible, it is necessary first to extract the juice from the hips. This does make rose hips particularly well suited to jelly-making—cooking them first and pouring through a jelly bag leaves all the unwanted pulp behind.

1 Place the rose hips and the apples in a preserving pan. Add enough water to cover them and simmer gently for around 45 minutes, until the fruit is soft and pulpy. Mash the fruit with the back of a spoon, then pour it into a jelly bag and leave undisturbed overnight, collecting the drips underneath in a measuring pitcher.

2 Allow ¾ cup sugar to every 1 cup juice. Place the juice in a preserving pan, add the warmed sugar, and stir over a low heat until all the sugar has dissolved, then turn up the heat and boil rapidly to reach setting point (see page 10). Skim if necessary (see page 11).

3 Pour the jelly into hot, sterilized jars (see page 8) and seal (see page 11).

rowan jelly

Rowan berries come from the European mountain ash (*Sorbus aucuparia*) and make a well-set jelly. Their slightly bitter flavor is offset by apples or quinces, making it ideal for serving with game.

Use equal amounts of rowan berries and apples, or quinces, if you have some, for this jelly. Make it in the same way as the Rose hip Jelly. Since this preserve is often served with rich meats, adding chopped rosemary to the jelly before packing works well, although it is inclined to settle at the bottom of the jars.

For quantity, see page 12
2 pounds crab apples, roughly chopped
sugar (for quantity see step 4)

crab apple jelly

Crab apples seem like such a neglected fruit, yet in season they are often abundant. Their small size makes them far too difficult to peel and core, so you either make them into jelly or purée the fruit for curds, fruit butters, or pie fillings. When making jelly, the idea is to end up with something that is as clear as can be.

Different apples will produce jellies in different shades, from amber to rose, and they always look beautiful when the light shines through them. For a spicier version, add a few cloves, a cinnamon stick, or some slices of gingerroot to the fruit at the start of cooking. However, I much prefer the single flavor of the fruit to sing through.

1 Place the apples in a preserving pan with 2 cups water. Simmer for about 45 minutes until the fruits have softened and turned fluffy, mashing them with a wooden spoon.

2 Place the apples in a jelly bag suspended over a measuring pitcher to catch the drips. Allow the apples to drain naturally for several hours or overnight—don't be tempted to squeeze the bag, if you want your jelly to be beautifully clear.

3 To extract more juice, remove the pulp from the bag, place in a pan with 1¼ cups water, and bring it to the boil again. Return it to the bag and allow to drain again for a few hours.

4 Allow ¾ cup sugar to every 1 cup of juice. Add the sugar to the juice, stirring over a low heat until the sugar has completely dissolved. Turn up the heat and boil rapidly to reach setting point (see page 10).

5 Skim if necessary (see page 11). Pour the jelly into hot, sterilized jars (see page 8) and seal (see page 11).

For quantity, see page 12
1 pound apples
1 pound damsons
sugar (for quantity see step 4 of Crab
  Apple Jelly)

damson & apple jelly

Making damsons into a jelly is the perfect solution to the "stoning the fruit" problem, which is one of the most tedious aspects of this fruit. Let the jelly bag do the work.

Follow the instructions for Crab Apple Jelly, first cooking the apples in 2 cups water and then adding the damsons for the final 15 minutes. Pour the mixed fruits into a jelly bag and complete as before.

For quantity, see page 12
1 pound apples
1 pound sloes
sugar (for quantity see step 4 of Crab
  Apple Jelly)

sloe & apple jelly

Sloes added to an apple jelly give it an exquisite rosy hue and a lovely tart taste. This is another versatile preserve, which works with both sweet and savory food and can be served with meats and cheeses. Sloes are supposed to be best picked after the first frost.

Follow the instructions for Crab Apple Jelly, first cooking the apples in 2 cups water, then adding the sloes during the last 15 minutes of cooking time. Pour everything into a jelly bag and complete as before.

For quantity, see page 12
5 pints blackberries
juice of ½ small lemon
sugar (for quantity see step 3)

blackberry jelly

Children seem to love collecting blackberries, so put them to work gathering the fruit for this jelly. Often blackberry jelly has added spices, but I much prefer the real fruit taste to dominate, so here I have opted for the pure fruit, with just a hint of lemon to help it set.

1 Place the berries in a preserving pan with scant ½ cup water. Simmer the fruit for 5 minutes until soft, mashing the berries with a wooden spoon.

2 Pour the fruit into a jelly bag, suspended over a measuring pitcher to catch the drips, and leave for several hours or overnight until the pulp left in the bag is almost dry.

3 Allow ¾ cup sugar for every 1 cup of juice. Add the lemon juice to the blackberry juice and pour into a preserving pan. Add the sugar and stir over a gentle heat until it is completely dissolved, then turn up the heat and boil rapidly to reach setting point (see page 10).

4 Skim if necessary (see page 11). Pour the jelly into hot, sterilized jars (see page 8) and seal (see page 11).

raspberry jelly

This jelly is the most wondrous, jewel-like color and is superbly fruity, which makes it ideal for using as the filling in a layer cake. It also suits anyone who likes raspberries but hates their seeds.

Follow the instructions for Blackberry Jelly, substituting raspberries for the blackberries.

marmalades

"Marmalade" usually refers to a preserve made from citrus fruits, served with toast at breakfast. Bitter Seville oranges make the best traditional citrus marmalade. However, the first marmalade was made from quinces and had Portuguese origins, while in France marmalade is made from other puréed fruits.

Makes about 4 cups
1½ pints black currants
1 pound apples, cut into large chunks
warmed sugar (see page 10; for quantity
    see step 3)

apple & black currant marmalade

Although this marmalade doesn't contain any citrus fruits, the black currants give just the right amount of tartness and punch to make it perfect for serving at breakfast. Processing the fruits through a food mill makes the most use of the fruit with very little preparation; there is no need to peel and core the apples at the beginning, since the food mill separates these from the flesh later to leave a purée with some texture in it.

As is often the case, when there are apples available, there is usually an abundant supply, and this is another great way of finding a use for an apple glut. Windfalls will do the job nicely, as this recipe doesn't call for perfect specimens.

1 Strip the black currants from their stalks by running the tines of a fork over the stems.

2 Place all the fruit together in a pan with 3 tablespoons water (just enough to keep the fruit from catching on the bottom of the pan). Simmer gently until the fruit is soft, the juices flow, and the apples are fluffy. Remove from the heat and leave until cool enough to handle.

3 Press the fruit mixture through the fine disk of a food mill, or a sieve, into a bowl. Measure the purée, then pour it into a preserving pan and add an equal volume of warmed sugar. Stir over a low heat until all the sugar has dissolved, then turn up the heat and boil rapidly to reach setting point (see page 10). Skim if necessary (see page 11).

4 Pour the marmalade into hot, sterilized jars (see page 8) and seal (see page 11).

apple & cranberry marmalade

This variation on the previous recipe illustrates the supreme versatility of apples and how they will blend with just about any fruit. Using this template, you can combine whatever fruits you have a plentiful supply of, using them half and half with apples, cook, and process to a purée, then match the volume in sugar. Make this marmalade using crab apples or a variety of cooking apple with a sharp flavor and offset them with another tangy fruit.

Follow the recipe for Apple & Black Currant Marmalade, substituting cranberries for the black currants.

Makes about 6 cups
2 pounds Seville oranges

1 small lemon
6 cups sugar

seville orange marmalade

Seville oranges are available for a short time only, in late winter, but they do make the best marmalade, which makes finding them worth the effort. Because of their extremely bitter taste, they are used only for cooking, but it is this robust quality that makes them particularly good when cooked and sweetened. You are either a cut-rind person or a smooth marmalade person, but shreds of perfectly cooked sweetened rind suspended in this amber jelly get my vote any day.

1 Preheat the oven to 350°F. Place the whole fruits in a heavy, lidded casserole or a preserving pan that will fit in the oven. Pour in 5 cups of water and bring it to simmering point on the cooktop.

2 Cover the pan (if using a preserving pan, make a lid from aluminum foil), and place in the oven. Poach the fruit for 2½–3 hours, by which time the skins will be soft.

3 Using a spoon, lift the fruit out of the liquid into a colander. When cool enough to handle, cut each fruit in half and scoop out the pulp with a spoon, leaving just the peel, placing the pulp, pith, and seeds in a muslin bag suspended over a bowl to catch any drips. (Alternatively, use a large piece of muslin gathered into a bag and tied with string). Measure the liquid, adding any collected in the bowl under the drained pulp, and if necessary add water to make it up to 1 quart.

4 Place the muslin bag in a saucepan with enough poaching liquid to cover. Bring to the boil and simmer for 15 minutes. Leave until cool enough to handle, then squeeze the bag to get as much of the liquid as possible from the pulp. Discard the bag and its contents.

5 Chop the rind into thin strips and put into a preserving pan. Add all the poaching liquid. If the mixture is cold, you can add the sugar without warming it; otherwise you will need to warm the sugar first (see page 10). Stir the sugar into the orange liquid over a low heat until it is completely dissolved and the liquid is clear, then boil rapidly for 15 minutes and test for setting point (see page 10).

6 Turn off the heat and leave the marmalade to stand for 15 minutes, then stir to distribute the peel. Skim if necessary (see page 11). Pour into hot, sterilized jars (see page 8) and seal (see page 11).

Makes about 5 cups
1 pound dried figs

3 lemons
4¾ cups warmed sugar (see page 10)

lemon & fig marmalade

This unusual combination is well worth trying. The lemon half-moons are left in large chunks, which give a lovely candied tang to the preserve. Along with the figs, they make a great start to the day.

1 Remove the stalks from the figs and cut each into 4 chunks. Halve the lemons lengthwise, then slice the halves thinly, collecting all the juice and any seeds. Place the seeds in a piece of muslin and tie it into a bag with string. Place the lemon slices and juice, the figs, and the wrapped seeds in a large bowl, cover them with 1 quart water and leave for 24 hours.

2 Pour the mixture into a pan and heat to simmering; leave simmering for 1–1½ hours until the lemon rind is soft. Leave to cool slightly and remove the seeds.

3 Add the warmed sugar. Stir over a low heat, without boiling, until the sugar has completely dissolved, then bring the marmalade to a rapid boil and cook until it reaches setting point (see page 10). Skim if necessary (see page 11). Pot into hot, sterilized jars (see page 8) and seal (see page 11).

Makes about 3¼ cups
juice and pared rind of 12 limes
3 cups warmed sugar (see page 10)

lime marmalade

If you want a change from traditional orange marmalade, this is the recipe to try. Here is another useful marmalade that can be made at any time of year using store-bought fruit. It has great color and flavor.

Shred the rind pieces finely. Place the pith and seeds from the limes in a piece of muslin and tie it up with string. Put the lime rind, lime juice, and 7 cups of water into a preserving pan and bring to the boil, then simmer for 1 hour until the rind is soft. Add the warmed sugar and stir over a low heat until all the sugar has dissolved, then turn up the heat and boil rapidly to reach setting point (see page 10). Remove the muslin bag, then pour the marmalade into warm, sterilized jars (see page 8) and seal (see page 11).

Makes about 4 cups
2 pounds peaches, roughly chopped
3¼ cups sugar

peach marmalade

I usually choose a tangy citrus preserve to spread on my toast at breakfast, but this aromatic, slightly gentler marmalade makes a lovely start to the day. You can, of course, eat it any time, but it has become one of my morning favorites. The cooking brings out the superb aroma of the fruit; and the variation below, including vanilla, produces an even more sybaritic experience.

1 Place the peaches and their stones in a pan along with 1 cup water. Bring them to simmering point and simmer until the peach pieces are soft.

2 Discard the stones and press the flesh through the fine disk of a food mill, or a sieve, to give a purée.

3 Put the purée into a preserving pan, add the sugar, warmed if necessary (see page 65, step 5), and stir gently over a low heat until the sugar has completely dissolved. Turn up the heat and boil until it reaches setting point (see page 10). Skim if necessary (see page 11).

4 Pour the marmalade into hot, sterilized jars (see page 8) and seal (see page 11).

peach & vanilla marmalade

Vanilla adds an unmistakable flavor to this breakfast classic. Peaches are wonderfully fragrant, anyway, and with added vanilla they become positively heavenly. The sticky black seeds scraped from the vanilla bean disperse throughout the preserve. Perfect on toast for breakfast, it's also an ideal sweet treat for any time of the day.

Split a vanilla bean lengthwise and add it to the peaches when cooking them with the water, as above. Remove the bean before puréeing the fruit and scrape the seeds from the bean pieces, using the sharp point of a knife. Stir the seeds into the peach purée and discard the bean pieces. Continue as above.

Makes about 4¼ cups
2 pounds quinces, fur washed off
3 small oranges

warmed sugar (see page 10; for quantity
see step 5)

quince & orange marmalade

Reputedly, the original marmalade was a preserve made from quinces, and the name comes from the word *marmelo*, the Portuguese word for this fruit. Quince seems to be a long-forgotten fruit, not often found for sale, although you may come across it in Mediterranean food stores. If you have a quince tree, use these wonderful fruits with orange to make a delicious marmalade. The quinces are cooked very slowly to intensify their flavor and bring out the best in them—use the oven on the lowest setting, or cook the marmalade in a slow cooker for a similar result.

1 Place the fruits in a lidded casserole dish (use a second casserole if they won't all fit into one) and pour in enough boiling water to cover the fruits so they just begin to float. Put on the lid and slow cook in the oven for 6–8 hours, or overnight, or cook in a slow cooker.

2 Remove from the oven and leave until cool enough to handle. Strain the liquid through a colander into a pan. Peel the quinces, quarter them, and remove the cores, then place the skins and cores in with the cooking liquid. Cut 2 of the oranges in half, scoop out the flesh, and add the seeds and pith to the liquid as well. Put the peel to one side.

3 Bring the mixture to the boil and reduce it down to about a third or a half of the original quantity. Pour the reduced mixture through a sieve into a preserving pan.

4 Cut the quinces into chunky slices about ¾ inch in diameter and ½ inch thick. Slice the whole orange into thin rounds and chop the empty orange halves into fine shreds.

5 Measure the quinces, orange slices, and shredded rind, add them to the reduced mixture, and warm through. Add the same volume of warmed sugar and stir over a low heat until all the sugar has dissolved, taking care to keep the orange slices intact, then turn up the heat and boil rapidly to reach setting point (see page 10). Skim if necessary (see page 11).

6 Remove the orange slices with a slotted spoon and use them to decorate the insides of the hot, sterilized jars (see page 8) by standing them on end against the glass. Pour the marmalade into the jars and seal (see page 11).

curds

These little pots of fruity loveliness are totally delicious. I make a selection of curds and serve them in teaspoon-sized dollops in bite-sized sweet pastry cases. Each one can be savored, discussed, and relished with due ceremony. Fruit curds don't keep quite so well as jams, but they won't hang around long enough anyway.

Makes about 3 cups
1 vanilla bean
1¼ pounds crab apples, halved, or cooking apples cut roughly into chunks

1 stick butter, preferably unsalted, cut into cubes
1⅞ cups fine granulated sugar
3 large eggs plus 2 egg yolks, beaten

crab apple & vanilla curd

Crab apples have just the right amount of tartness to give this curd lots of flavor, but any sharp apples will do the job just as well. Because the fruit is puréed, there isn't much preparation needed, so windfalls can be used, if desired, more or less as they are (just with any bad bits removed). This curd makes the most fabulous filling for a sweet pastry case.

1 Split the vanilla bean lengthwise and place it with the apples in a pan, adding 1 tablespoon water. Simmer gently until the apples are soft, stirring occasionally to be sure the fruit doesn't catch on the bottom of the pan. Remove it from the heat and leave to cool.

2 Remove the vanilla bean, then purée the apples by pressing them through the fine disk of a food mill or a sieve, collecting the resulting purée in a bowl. Scrape the seeds from the vanilla bean pieces with a sharp knife and add them to the apples along with the bean. Add the other ingredients, pouring the egg through a sieve.

3 Place the bowl over a pan of simmering water (or use a double boiler) and heat gently, stirring all the time until everything is blended and the curd begins to thicken and coats the back of the spoon. This stage should take about 20–30 minutes.

4 Remove the vanilla bean pieces. Pour the hot curd into small, hot, sterilized jars (see page 8) and seal (see page 11).

Makes about 1½ cups
½ pound apricots, quartered and stoned
2 eggs, well beaten
zest and juice of 1 lemon

3 tbsp (slightly rounded) butter,
    preferably unsalted, cut into cubes
1 scant cup fine granulated sugar

apricot curd

Fresh homegrown apricots cannot be bettered, but even commercially grown ones from the supermarket will make tasty curd. Choose the best-quality organic eggs when making curds, as they also help to give a brighter color to the finished product.

1 Place the apricots in a pan with 2 tablespoons water (just enough to stop the fruit from catching on the bottom of the pan) and cook gently until soft.

2 Cool the fruit slightly, then press it through the fine disk of a food mill or a sieve, collecting the resulting purée in a bowl.

3 Strain the beaten eggs through a sieve into the purée. Add the lemon zest and juice, the butter, and the sugar.

4 Place the bowl over a pan of simmering water (or use a double boiler). Cook gently, stirring continuously with a wooden spoon, until the mixture is completely blended and thickens enough to coat the back of the spoon. This should take about 30 minutes.

5 Pour the curd into small, hot, sterilized jars (see page 8) and seal (see page 11).

Makes about 1 cup
1 pint raspberries
⅝ (rounded) cup fine granulated sugar

3 tbsp butter, preferably unsalted,
 cut into cubes
2 small eggs, beaten

raspberry curd

Raspberries give this delicious curd a wonderful color and a lovely tangy taste. Save small unusual-shaped glass jars especially for making curds. They are great to give as presents.

1 Place the raspberries in a pan and cook gently for 5–10 minutes, squashing the fruits with a spoon to help release the juice.

2 Push the fruit through a sieve, collecting the purée in a bowl.

3 Place the bowl over a pan of simmering water (or use a double boiler) and add all the other ingredients, pouring the beaten eggs through a sieve onto the purée. Stir with a wooden spoon until everything is well blended. Continue cooking, stirring constantly, until the curd is thick enough to coat the back of the spoon—this should take about 20–30 minutes.

4 Pour the curd into small, hot, sterilized jars (see page 8) and seal (see page 11).

Makes about 2 cups
1 pint blueberries
zest and juice of 1 large lime

4 tbsp butter, preferably unsalted,
 cut into cubes
1⅛ cups fine granulated sugar
2 large eggs, beaten

blueberry & lime curd

The best and tastiest blueberries err on the tart side, and here these berries are given an extra boost of flavor with the addition of the zest and juice of a lime.

Place the blueberries in a pan with the lime zest and juice, and cook gently for 5–10 minutes until tender. Purée the fruit and continue as for steps 2–4 of Raspberry Curd.

Makes about 2 cups
1 pint gooseberries, with any large
　　stems removed
zest of 1 lime
6 tbsp plus 1 tsp butter, preferably
　　unsalted, cut into cubes
⅞ cup fine granulated sugar
3 large eggs plus 2 yolks, beaten

gooseberry curd

Gooseberries are not always that easy to find in American grocery stores, but they are relatively easy to grow and don't need much attention to flourish. Try growing some so you can make this curd.

1 Place the gooseberries in a pan with ⅜ cup water and cook gently for 5–10 minutes, squashing the fruits with a spoon to help release the juice.

2 Press the fruit through the fine disk of a food mill, or a sieve, to remove the skins and seeds, collecting the purée in a bowl.

3 Place the bowl over a pan of simmering water (or use a double boiler) and add all the other ingredients, pouring the beaten eggs through a sieve onto the purée. Continue stirring with a wooden spoon until everything becomes well blended and smooth and thick enough to coat the back of the spoon—this should take about 20–30 minutes.

4 Pour the curd into hot, sterilized jars (see page 8) and seal (see page 11).

Makes about 1¼ cups
zest and juice of 3 lemons
6 tbsp butter, preferably unsalted,
   cut into cubes

⅞ cup fine granulated sugar
3 large eggs, beaten

lemon curd

An outstanding classic, this sharp lemon curd makes the perfect filling for an open tart. It can also be spread between the layers of a cake, or swirled through vanilla ice cream. Utter perfection, whichever way you serve it.

1 Place the lemon zest and juice in a bowl set over a pan of simmering water (or use a double boiler) along with the butter and sugar. Add the beaten eggs, pouring them through a sieve.

2 Stir with a wooden spoon until everything becomes heated through and well blended. Continue cooking, stirring constantly, until the curd thickens enough to coat the back of the spoon—this should take about 15–20 minutes.

3 Pour the curd into small, hot, sterilized jars (see page 8), seal (see page 11).

Makes about 1 cup
zest and juice of 3 Seville oranges
3 tbsp (slightly rounded) butter, preferably
   unsalted, cut into cubes

¾ cup fine granulated sugar
2 large eggs, beaten

bitter orange curd

The bitter nature of Seville oranges works perfectly for a curd. Most sweet oranges just don't have enough character to use in this way, although blood oranges have more of a flavor kick than other sweet varieties, so they work well also. Use the curd as a filling for a sweet pastry tart, or spread it liberally between the layers of a rich chocolate cake, or simply serve it on a thick slice of fresh bread.

Follow the instructions for making Lemon Curd using the ingredients above.

Makes about 1¼ cups
zest of 2 small grapefruit
6 tbsp grapefruit juice

6 tbsp butter, preferably unsalted,
    cut into cubes
⅞ cup fine granulated sugar
3 large eggs, beaten

grapefruit curd

Here's another citrus variation on the lemon curd theme. This curd is smooth and creamy but still has its own distinctive tang.

Follow the instructions for making Lemon Curd using the ingredients above.

Makes about 1½ cups

1 small butternut squash, peeled, deseeded and roughly chopped

zest and juice of 1 lemon

zest and juice of 1 orange

4 tbsp plus 1 tsp butter, preferably unsalted, cut into cubes

⅞ cup fine granulated sugar

2 large eggs plus 2 yolks, beaten

4 pieces of stem ginger, approx. 1 inch in diameter, finely chopped

3 tbsp syrup from the stem ginger

butternut & ginger curd

Squashes and pumpkins are naturally sweet, so ideal for making into sweet preserves. Here butternut squash is the main ingredient, but other types can be used instead. The brighter orange the flesh, the better. Chopped pieces of stem ginger add a lovely bite to the texture.

1 Place the squash in a pan with ½ cup water to stop it from sticking to the pan as it cooks. Cover and cook until soft, then pour off any excess liquid.

2 Purée the squash in a food processor or pass it through the fine disk of a food mill. Alternatively, press it through a sieve.

3 Measure out 1¼ cups of the squash purée and place this in a bowl over simmering water (or use a double boiler), along with all the other ingredients, pouring the beaten eggs through a sieve onto the purée. Continue stirring with a wooden spoon until everything becomes well blended, the sugar is dissolved, and the curd thickens and will coat the back of the spoon—this should take about 30 minutes.

4 Pour the curd into small, hot, sterilized jars (see page 8) and seal (see page 11).

nectars

Nectars and syrups are, in fact, the same thing. These sweetened fruity concentrates are delicious, not only diluted with water but added to milk for milk shakes, poured over ice cream, or swirled through cake batter prior to baking for a marbled effect. At best, they really capture the essence of the fruit.

Makes about 3 cups
3 pints overripe black currants
sugar (for quantity, see step 3)

black currant nectar

Another fruit rich in vitamin C, black currants are an ideal fruit for making into a nectar, which can then be diluted as a cold drink or a hot comforting drink—similar to, but better than, the ready-made kind available in delicatessens.

1 Strip the black currants from their stalks by running the tines of a fork over the stems.

2 Place them with 1¾ cups water in the top of a double boiler or in a bowl over a pan of simmering water and cook for half an hour, stirring occasionally and mashing the fruit with the back of the spoon. Then strain through a sieve into a measuring pitcher; discard the pulp.

3 Add 2 cups sugar to every 2½ cups juice and stir over a low heat until all the sugar has dissolved. Bring just to the boil, then quickly remove from the heat.

4 Pour the nectar into clean, clip-top or corked bottles and sterilize (see pages 13–14), or pour into freezer containers, seal, and freeze.

damson nectar

Freshly picked damsons make a sublime and unusual nectar bursting with tart flavor. Drizzle over yogurt or ice cream.

Follow the recipe for Black Currant Nectar, substituting 2 pounds of damsons for the black currants.

Makes about 6½ cups
20 heads of elderflower
6½ cups fine granulated sugar
⅓ cup citric acid
2 lemons, thinly sliced
2 oranges, thinly sliced

elderflower nectar

The shrubby elder (*Sambucus nigra*) is so common in the countryside that it is easy to pass it by without a second look. Yet in early summer it provides one of the most distinctive ingredients of the preserving year—one that can be foraged for free. The heavily scented blossoms make a refreshing nectar that you can dilute with still or sparkling mineral water. The fragrance, as well as the taste, evokes lazy summer afternoons. Gather the flower heads on dry, sunny days, away from busy roads, and select flower heads that are fresh and white, avoiding older creamy yellow blossoms. This delicious nectar will keep for around 2 months in the fridge; if frozen in plastic containers, it will last for a year or more—so be sure to make plenty.

1 Shake the flowers, face down, to remove any unwanted creatures.

2 Place the sugar and 5 cups water in a stainless steel or enamel pan and warm slowly, stirring, to dissolve the sugar completely, then bring the resulting syrup to a boil.

3 Add the flowers, bring again to the boil, then remove from the heat.

4 Add the other ingredients, stir well, then leave, covered, in a cool place for 24 hours.

5 Strain the cordial into clean, clip-top or corked bottles and sterilize (see pages 13–14).

Makes about 3 cups
2 pieces or fresh gingerroot, bruised, each about ¾ x 2½ inches

juice and thinly pared zest of 2 lemons
sugar (for quantity see step 2)

ginger & lemon nectar

Although not intentionally medicinal, this nectar is soothing and warming and is ideal to drink as a hot beverage if you feel a cold coming on.

1 Place the ginger and lemon zest in a pan with 5 cups water. Simmer gently for 40 minutes. Strain through a sieve into a measuring pitcher; discard the zest and ginger.

2 Add the lemon juice to the ginger-infused juice. Add ⅝ cup sugar for every 1 cup liquid and stir over a low heat until all the sugar has dissolved. Bring just to the boil, then quickly remove from the heat.

3 Pour the nectar into clean, clip-top or corked bottles and sterilize (see pages 13–14), or pour into freezer containers, seal, and freeze.

Makes about 2 quarts
8–10 lemons
6–8 oranges

3 scant cups sugar
½ tsp citric acid

lemon & orange nectar

This classic fresh citrus nectar is so versatile that you can drink it any time. It makes a drink like the best old-fashioned lemonade mixed with orangeade.

Pare the zest finely from 1 lemon and 1 orange. Put the sugar, zest and 2½ cups water into a pan. Heat gently to make a syrup, then boil for 5 minutes. Strain through a sieve into a measuring pitcher; discard the zest. Squeeze enough lemons and oranges to produce the same amount of juice as syrup, keeping the same proportions of half lemon, half orange. Mix the syrup and fruit juices together in the pan and add the citric acid, stirring until it has dissolved. Bottle as above.

Makes about 2½ cups
4 cups rose hips, freshly gathered
sugar (for quantity see step 5)

rose hip nectar

Rose hips are one of the most popular foraged fruits, offered for free from nature's larder. They are the fruit of the wild rose, and gathering them is all part of the fun. They should be picked fully ripe, when a deep red color, and preferably after the first frosts, which soften them. If picked a little earlier, they can be placed, freshly picked, in the freezer overnight to give the same result as if they had been nipped by the frost. Rose hip nectar has a high vitamin C content and is so sweet and delicious that it is a great way of encouraging children to boost their vitamin intake effortlessly.

1 Place the rose hips in a pan and mash them with the back of a spoon to break them down. Pour boiling water over them, to cover, and simmer for 5 minutes until the hips are soft.

2 Remove the pan from the heat and leave to stand for 15 minutes, then strain the mixture through a jelly bag, collecting the juice in a measuring pitcher. Set the juice aside.

3 Remove the pulp from the jelly bag and place it in the pan. Add 2 cups water and bring the mixture to the boil, then repeat step 2, but this time squeezing out the excess liquid from the pulp.

4 Combine both pitchers of juice in the pan and boil the mixture to reduce it by approximately a third to a half.

5 Add ½ rounded cup sugar for every 1 cup juice and stir over a low heat until all the sugar has dissolved. Bring just to the boil, then remove quickly from the heat.

6 Pour the nectar into clean, clip-top or corked bottles and sterilize (see pages 13–14), or pour into freezer containers, seal, and freeze.

Makes about 2¼ cups
4 pints overripe raspberries
sugar (for quantity see step 2)

raspberry nectar

Raspberry nectar makes a lovely alternative to a dollop of jam on rice pudding, for example. Unlike preserves, which often benefit from being made with combinations of flavors, nectars are usually best when made with a single fruit, thus showcasing the individual characteristics of that fruit.

1 Place the raspberries in the top of a double boiler, or in a bowl over a pan of simmering water. Mash the berries with the back of a spoon to break them down and add 1 tablespoon water, then cook until the fruit is soft, the juices are flowing, and the fruit comes to the boil, stirring now and then. Pour into a jelly bag and collect the drips in a measuring pitcher.

2 Add 1 scant ¾ cup sugar to every 1 cup juice and stir over a low heat until all the sugar has dissolved. Bring just to the boil, then quickly remove from the heat.

3 Pour the nectar into clean, clip-top or corked bottles and sterilize (see pages 13–14), or pour into freezer containers, seal, and freeze.

Makes about 4½ cups
2⅓ cups sugar

2 pounds overripe apricots,
halved and stoned

apricot nectar

Another lush and fruity treat to dilute into a refreshing summer drink. Even if there aren't many apricots to go around, making just a small amount of this nectar is well worth while.

Put the sugar and 4½ cups water in a pan and heat gently to make a syrup. Add the apricots to the syrup, simmering until the fruit pieces are tender. Strain through a sieve into a measuring pitcher. (Do not discard the apricots. Instead, use them as a delicious pie filling, or serve them with cream.) Pour the nectar into clean, clip-top or corked bottles and sterilize (see pages 13–14), or pour into freezer containers, seal, and freeze.

strawberry nectar

The vibrant color and evocative scent of this syrup shout out "summer." If possible, choose homegrown or locally grown fruit, so the berries are at their freshest and sweetest.

Follow the recipe for Raspberry Nectar, substituting strawberries for the raspberries.

Makes about 2 cups
3 pints overripe blackberries
sugar (for quantity see step 2)

blackberry nectar

Try this nectar as an alternative to crème de cassis in a Kir cocktail—or even, using sparkling instead of still white wine, for a Kir royale.

1 Place the blackberries with ½ cup water in the top of a double boiler, or in a bowl over a pan of simmering water. Cook for 1 hour, stirring occasionally and mashing the fruit with the back of the spoon, then strain through a sieve into a measuring pitcher; discard the pulp.

2 Add ¾ cup sugar to every 1 cup juice and stir over a low heat until all the sugar has dissolved. Bring just to the boil, then quickly remove from the heat.

3 Pour the nectar into clean, clip-top or corked bottles and sterilize (see pages 13–14), or pour into freezer containers, seal, and freeze.

Makes about 2¼ cups
4 pints overripe mulberries
sugar (for quantity see below)

mulberry nectar

Gathering mulberries can be a hazardous occupation. The traditional method involves spreading a sheet on the ground underneath the branches and shaking the tree till the fruit drops.

Place the mulberries in the top of a double boiler or in a bowl over a pan of simmering water. Mash the fruits with the back of a spoon to break them down and add 1 tablespoon water. Cook until the fruit is soft and the juices are flowing and the fruit comes to the boil, stirring now and then. Pour into a jelly bag and collect the drips in a measuring pitcher. Add ⅝ rounded cup sugar to every 1 cup juice and stir over a low heat until all the sugar has dissolved. Bring just to the boil, then quickly remove from the heat. Bottle as above.

Makes about 3 cups
2½ pints overripe red currants
3 overripe nectarines (approx. 1 pound
   in weight), halved, stoned and diced
sugar (for quantity see step 3)

red currant & nectarine nectar

Red currants and nectarines make a colorful nectar that tastes great too. Like other nectars, it can be poured into juice pop molds and frozen.

1 Strip the red currants from their stalks—the simplest and quickest way is to run the tines of a fork over the stems.

2 Place the nectarines in the top of a double boiler or in a bowl over a pan of simmering water. Mash the fruits with the back of a spoon to break them down and add ½ cup water. Cook until the fruit is soft, then add the red currants and continue to cook until they are soft and the juice is flowing. Strain through a sieve into a measuring pitcher; discard the pulp.

3 Add ⅝ rounded cup sugar to every 1 cup juice and stir over a low heat until all the sugar has dissolved. Bring just to the boil, then quickly remove from the heat.

4 Pour the nectar into clean, clip-top or corked bottles and sterilize (see pages 13–14), or pour into freezer containers, seal, and freeze. To make juice pops, use purchased pop molds.

fruits in syrup

Before the advent of the freezer, bottling fruits and vegetables in water or sugar syrup was the usual way to preserve them. Now that bottling has become a niche activity and freezing the norm, fruits in syrup have taken on an altogether more luxurious feel. Packed in neat jars and spiced or flavored, they make superb presents.

Makes about 1½ pints
1¾ cups sugar
pared rind and juice of 1 small orange
1 small cinnamon stick

4 cardamom pods, with seeds crushed
2 star anise
1½ pounds apricots, halved and stoned

apricots in syrup

This is a lovely way of using up any luscious apricots that come your way. The syrup is quite spicy and helps make this bottled fruit very special—special enough to serve alone as dessert at the end of a meal. Leaving the whole spices in the jar means it looks good, too.

1 Make a syrup by placing 2½ cups water in a pan with the sugar, 3 strips of the orange zest plus the juice of the orange and the spices. Heat gently, stirring to dissolve the sugar before turning up the heat and bringing to a simmer.

2 Add the apricots and poach them until they are cooked but still in whole pieces, then remove them with a slotted spoon and pack them into hot, sterilized jars (see page 11). Bring the syrup to the boil and boil rapidly for 10–15 minutes to thicken and reduce it.

3 Pour the syrup and spices over the fruit to cover completely. Gently tap the jars to release any air bubbles, then seal (see page 11).

nectarines in syrup

One of summer's most delectable fruits, nectarines also make a special treat when preserved, ready to "encore" in fall or winter.

Substitute the same quantity of nectarines for the apricots in Apricots in Syrup. Medium-sized fruits can be used halved with the stones removed; but larger fruits should be cut into quarters. Proceed as for main recipe.

damsons in syrup

Since the damsons are kept whole, you might like to warn anyone eating them to beware of the stones. It is a small price to pay for this delicious preserve.

Use damsons in place of apricots, but leave the fruits whole. Poach them gently in the syrup, removing them as soon as you see signs of the skins' splitting. Damsons almost always have such a superb flavor that too many spices will only spoil them. So keep the orange peel and juice but omit the spices in Apricots in Syrup. A darker sugar will also suit this fruit, so use demerara or good quality dark brown sugar instead of white sugar.

Makes about 1 pint
¼ scant cup sugar
½ vanilla bean

approx. 1¼-inch piece of cinnamon stick
6 or 7 figs, halved
¼ tsp citric acid

figs in vanilla syrup

These gorgeous fruits look magnificent in the jar, beautifully pink and jewel-like. Baking the jar in the oven will help the figs to keep.

1 Preheat the oven to 300°F. Place the sugar, vanilla bean, and cinnamon stick in a pan and add 1 cup water. Stir over a low heat to dissolve the sugar, then bring to the boil and simmer for 2 minutes to make a syrup. Remove from the heat. Discard the cinnamon stick. Slice the vanilla bean in half lengthwise, scrape out the seeds with a knife, and add them to the syrup.

2 Pack the figs into a clean, sterilized jar (see page 8) with the cut sides facing outward. Push the vanilla bean halves among the figs. Pour the syrup over the figs to fill the jar, swiveling the jar to remove any air bubbles.

3 Wrap aluminum foil over the top of the jar and place it in the oven, on a baking tray lined with several layers of folded newspaper. Bake for 25–30 minutes, by which time the syrup will have turned a lovely shade of pink. Remove from the oven, discard the foil, and seal.

Makes about 1 quart
6 oranges, cut into ¼-inch slices
1¾ cups white wine vinegar
1¼ (rounded) cups sugar

⅓ cup clear, pale honey
1 small cinnamon stick
2 tsp whole coriander seeds
1 tsp whole cloves

orange slices in spiced honey

Using a medley of spices as flavoring, and honey as the sweetener, makes a delicious and aromatic syrup for these orange slices.

Place the orange slices in a pan with just enough water to cover. Bring to the boil and simmer for 1 hour until the zest is tender. Strain off the water and discard. Put all other ingredients in a pan and heat gently, stirring, to dissolve the sugar and honey. Add the oranges, simmer for 30 minutes until the zest is translucent, then pack into sterilized jars (see page 8). Strain the syrup to remove the spices, then return to the pan and boil rapidly for 10 minutes to reduce. Pour into the jars to the brim, then seal.

Makes about 1 quart
2 pounds small peaches (approx. 9 peaches)
1¼ (rounded) cups sugar
1 vanilla bean (optional)
approx. 1 cup brandy

whole peaches in brandy

Preserving peaches in a brandy syrup is a great way to use up peaches being sold off cheaply at the supermarket. Quite often you find them still firm and perfect but having reached their sell-by date and thus a bargain. Of course if you grow your own peaches, even better! Packed into a jar, they make a wonderful present, which looks very impressive. Including a vanilla bean is optional, but it is a resourceful way of using up beans that have already had their seeds removed for other recipes, and they look good showing through the jar. This recipe makes enough to fill one big jar, so adapt quantities if you want to use smaller jars.

1 Skin the peaches by plunging them in boiling water for a couple of minutes. You may need to do this in batches. The skins should peel away easily from the fruits, using a sharp knife.

2 Place 1¾ cups water in a pan with half of the sugar and stir over a low heat to dissolve the sugar. Bring the syrup to a simmer and add the vanilla bean, if using.

3 Add the skinned peaches to the syrup, probably in 3 batches, and poach for 5 minutes, spooning the syrup over them if it doesn't cover them. Remove with a slotted spoon and place in a clean, sterilized jar (see page 8), packing them in neatly but taking care not to squash or damage them. Remove the bean from the syrup and push it down among the fruits.

4 Add the remaining sugar to the syrup in the pan and stir until all the sugar has dissolved, then turn up the heat and boil rapidly for 4 minutes. Remove from the heat and leave to cool for 10 minutes.

5 Measure the syrup, add the same amount of brandy, and stir together. Pour the brandy syrup over the peaches to cover, then seal the jar (see page 11).

greengages in brandy

Greengage plums have a great color and an aromatic flavor that works really well here. Any brandy left over in the jar after dishing up the fruit can be drunk like a liqueur. Don't waste a drop!

Follow the recipe for Whole Peaches in Brandy, substituting 2 pounds of firm, ripe greengages for the peaches. There is no need to skin the greengages. Be careful when poaching the fruits that they stay whole, and remove them immediately from the syrup if they show signs of splitting.

Makes about 1 quart
3 cups ripe cherries
⅜ cup sugar
2⅜ cups eau de vie

cherries in eau de vie

This has to be the easiest preserve in the book, and yet the minimal effort involved is rewarded with a truly luxurious result. Serve simply with whipped cream and enjoy.

1 Use a cherry stoner to pit the cherries and remove any stalks, then pack them into sterilized, wide-necked jars (see page 8), layering the fruits with sugar now and then. When the jars are filled with cherries, spoon any remaining sugar on top.

2 Pour the eau de vie over the cherries, filling the jars to the top, and seal. Store the jars for at least 6 weeks, giving them a shake from time to time to help dissolve the sugar and create a syrup.

chutneys

Chutney making is an inexact science, and you can adjust spices and sweetness to suit your tastes. It requires a long cooking time to reach a rich, thick constituency, but don't cook it until too dry as it will dry out slightly in storage—a shiny, moist chutney is what you are aiming for. You must be patient and leave chutneys to mature.

Makes about 4¼ cups

1 tsp. allspice
1 tsp. mustard seeds
1 tsp. ground coriander
1 small cinnamon stick
1 pound apricots, quartered and stoned
1 pound cooking apples, peeled, cored,
   and chopped into large chunks
3 cups cider or wine vinegar
1½ cups golden raisins, chopped
2 cloves garlic, peeled and chopped
rind and juice of 1 lemon
1 tsp. salt
¾-inch-square piece of fresh gingerroot,
   peeled and minced
2 cups warmed sugar (see page 10)

apricot chutney

This chutney can be made using either fresh or dried fruit. Here, the recipe uses fresh apricots, making the most of a seasonal glut. However, if you want to make it out of season, you can use dried apricots, instead. Simply replace the fresh apricots with 1⅔ cups dried apricots, soaked for a few hours in the vinegar, then proceed in the same way.

1 Place the spices in a piece of cheesecloth and tie it into a bag with string. Place the apricots, apples, vinegar, and spice bag in a stainless steel preserving pan and bring to the boil, then simmer for 10 minutes.

2 Add the other ingredients and stir over a low heat until all the sugar has dissolved, then bring to the boil and simmer for approximately 1½ hours until the chutney is thick but still juicy, stirring occasionally.

3 Remove the muslin bag, then pour the chutney into hot, sterilized jars (see page 8) and seal (see page 11).

apricot & orange chutney

Orange is a great companion to apricots and helps the chutney to be even more colorful. This recipe is another useful one, since it can be made at any time of year using dried apricots.

Replace the lemon in Apricot Chutney with 3 large oranges. Grate the zest from them and cut away and discard the white pith, then chop the orange flesh roughly. Add them in step 2 and continue as above.

Makes about 9 cups
2 pounds raw beets, peeled and
   coarsely grated
1 pound onions, peeled and chopped
1½ pounds cooking apples, peeled,
   cored, and chopped

3 cups seedless raisins
4½ cups malt vinegar or spiced pickling
   vinegar (see page 13)
4 scant cups sugar
2 tsp. ground ginger

beet chutney

Beets are another vegetable that can be overabundant at the height of the season, so chutney-making suits them well.

1 Place everything in a stainless steel preserving pan and stir over a gentle heat to dissolve the sugar. Bring to the boil, then simmer gently for about 1 hour until the beetroot and onions are soft and the chutney is thick but still juicy, stirring occasionally.

2 Pour the chutney into hot, sterilized jars (see page 8) and seal (see page 11).

Makes about 5¼ cups
1 pound zucchini
2 rounded tsp. salt, plus extra for sprinkling
1 pound scarlet runner beans, cut into
   ¾-inch pieces
½ pound corn kernels
1 pound onions, minced

2¾ cups cider vinegar
1 tbsp. cornstarch
1 tbsp. English mustard powder
1 tbsp. turmeric
1 green chili, deseeded and minced
2 cups warmed demerara sugar
   (see page 10)

vegetable garden chutney

This chutney is a great way of using up homegrown odds and ends—especially useful when produce is growing faster than you can consume it. Try other combinations of vegetables, too.

Cut the zucchini in half lengthwise, then into slices. Place in a bowl and sprinkle with salt, leave for 1 hour, then rinse the zucchini thoroughly and drain. Place all the vegetables and the vinegar in a stainless steel preserving pan. Bring to the boil, then simmer for 10 minutes. Mix the cornstarch, mustard, and turmeric in a bowl with a few spoonfuls of vinegar from the pan to form a smooth paste. Add the paste to the pan with the chili and warmed sugar and stir over a low heat until the sugar has dissolved, then simmer for ¾–1 hour until the chutney is thick but juicy, stirring occasionally. Pack as above.

Makes about 6 cups

2 pounds damsons
3¾ cups malt vinegar
1 small cinnamon stick
1 rounded tbsp. allspice
1 scant tsp. cloves
½ pound (generous) cooking apples,
  peeled, cored, and chopped
2 small onions, peeled and minced
1½ cups raisins
1½ cups chopped dates
3 cups (packed) soft brown sugar
2 small cloves garlic, peeled and crushed
1 tbsp. ground ginger
1 tbsp. coarse salt

damson chutney

This chutney is rich, dark, and heavenly. Damsons are one of my absolute favorite fruits for preserving and lend a superb flavor across the board to any jam, jelly, chutney, or pickle that uses them. Removing the stones is a laborious job but is always worth the time. My chosen technique is to cook the fruits first, then remove the stones by hand (usually with the pan on my lap in front of the television). This tedious task has now become part of the chutney-making tradition for me, and since damsons have only a short season once a year, it isn't such a hardship.

1 Place the damsons in a pan with 1 cup of the vinegar and cook them until they are soft and bursting. Leave until cool enough to handle, then remove the stones. Place the spices in a piece of muslin and tie it into a bag with string.

2 Place all the ingredients in a stainless steel preserving pan and bring to the boil, then simmer gently for 2–2½ hours until the chutney is dark and thick but still juicy, stirring from time to time.

3 Remove the muslin bag, then pour the chutney into hot, sterilized jars (see page 8) and seal (see page 11).

Makes about 5¼ cups
2 pounds green tomatoes
½ pound cooking apples, peeled and cored
1 pound red onions, roughly chopped
¾ cup rounded (packed) soft brown sugar
2½ cups malt vinegar

½ tsp. mustard seeds
½ tsp. cayenne pepper
1 tbsp. finely grated fresh gingerroot
1¼ cups raisins
3 green chilies, deseeded and minced
1 tsp. salt

green tomato & red onion chutney

At the end of the season, when there is no more heat left outside to ripen the last of the tomatoes, it is time to bring them into the house. If you place them on any empty windowsill you can find, there's a chance that the last precious fruits will slowly turn from green to red. Packing them in boxes, spaced apart in layers with straw or woolen material between them, is another way of ripening them gradually and prolonging the season; but if you have plenty to spare, the still-green ones are just perfect for turning into chutney.

1 To skin the tomatoes, place them in a bowl and pour boiling water over them, then leave for a minute or two. The skins should now slide off the fruits when you cut into them with a sharp knife. It is harder to remove the skins when tomatoes are green, so steeping them for longer than usual helps. Chop the tomatoes roughly.

2 Place all the ingredients in a stainless steel preserving pan and bring to the boil. Reduce the heat and simmer until everything is cooked and the chutney has thickened, stirring occasionally.

3 Pour the chutney into hot, sterilized jars (see page 8) and seal (see page 11).

Makes about 5¼ cups

2 pounds mango flesh, when peeled and
   stoned (about 4 pounds unstoned)
2 tsp. mixed pickling spices
juice and thickly pared rind of 1 small orange
½ pound onions, minced

1¼ cups white wine vinegar
2 cloves garlic
1 tbsp. grated gingerroot
2 hot red chilies, deseeded and minced
2⅝ cups (packed) warmed good-quality
   light brown sugar (see page 10)

mango chutney

A classic accompaniment to Indian food, this sticky sweet chutney is unbeatable. This is a great
way of using mangoes when slightly underripe, if, like me, you aren't ever quite sure whether
your mangoes are ripe enough to eat.

1 Cut half of the mango flesh into small pieces and leave the other half in larger
chunks. Put the pickling spices and rind pieces in a piece of muslin and tie it
into a bag.

2 Place all the ingredients except the sugar and large mango chunks in a
stainless steel preserving pan and simmer gently for 20 minutes until the mango
and onions are soft.

3 Add the rest of the mango and
simmer gently for another 5 minutes.
Add the warmed sugar and stir over
a low heat until it has completely
dissolved, then boil until the mixture
reaches a thick, jamlike consistency,
stirring gently and taking care to
retain the chunky texture.

4 Remove the muslin bag. Allow
the chutney to cool for 10 minutes,
then stir again to redistribute the bits.

5 Pour the chutney into hot,
sterilized jars (see page 8) and seal
(see page 11).

Makes about 5½ cups

2¼ pounds nectarines, skinned, stoned, and roughly chopped

½ pound cooking apples, peeled, cored, and chopped

½ pound onions, peeled and finely sliced

1½ cups raisins

1½ cups (packed) light brown sugar

3 tbsp. stem ginger, minced

2 cloves garlic

2 tsp. coarse salt

1 tsp. cayenne pepper

1 pint white wine vinegar

nectarine chutney

Nectarines work so well here. They have just the right amount of sweetness and tartness to make an excellent chutney and this recipe is a real favorite of mine. I like it with macaroni cheese, and I'll put it in a sandwich with just about anything!

1 Place all the ingredients in a stainless steel preserving pan and stir over a gentle heat to dissolve the sugar. Simmer gently for approximately 1½ hours until the chutney is thick but still juicy, stirring occasionally.

2 Pour the chutney into hot, sterilized jars (see page 8) and seal (see page 11).

peach chutney

Peaches make a straight and worthy substitute here when used instead of nectarines. Use whichever you have in plentiful supply and you won't be disappointed.

Follow the recipe for Nectarine Chutney, substituting peaches for the nectarines. Choose fruits that are firm and barely ripened.

Makes about 4 cups

2 pounds onions, peeled and finely sliced

2 scant tbsp. olive oil

1 pint red wine vinegar (or a mixture of red vine vinegar and balsamic vinegar)

3 cups (packed) good-quality brown sugar

2 bay leaves

15–18 black peppercorns, crushed

2 scant tsp. salt

onion marmalade

Really a chutney or relish, not a marmalade at all, onion marmalade has become very fashionable in Britain in recent years. Generally it isn't a great keeper, but this version, like other chutneys, will keep well.

1 Separate the onion slices into rings. Heat the oil in a stainless steel preserving pan, add the onion rings, and cook them gently for about 20 minutes until they are soft but not browned.

2 Add all the other ingredients and simmer gently for 1–1½ hours until the marmalade is dark and thick but still juicy, stirring occasionally.

3 Pour the marmalade into hot, sterilized jars (see page 8) and seal (see page 11).

Makes about 6¼ cups

1 tsp. whole allspice

1 tsp. coriander seeds

2 tsp. mustard seeds

½ tsp. cumin seeds

2 pieces fresh root ginger, approx.
  ¾ x 2½ inches, bruised

3¼ pounds red tomatoes, skinned
  and chopped

1 pound cooking apples, peeled, cored,
  and diced

1 pound onions, peeled and minced

2 small cloves garlic, peeled and minced

1 cup red wine vinegar

1 tsp. coarse salt

⅞ cup (packed) warmed good-quality
  brown sugar (see page 10)

red tomato & garlic chutney

This is another easy classic that uses up a glut of tomatoes. In fact, chutney is so easy to make that it is surprising that anyone ever buys the store-bought stuff. Here, the red fruits and brown sugar give the chutney a lovely rich color.

1 Place the whole spices and bruised ginger in a piece of muslin and tie it into a bag with string.

2 Place all the ingredients except the sugar in a stainless steel preserving pan and bring to the boil, then simmer until tender. Add the warmed sugar and stir over a low heat until all the sugar has dissolved. Turn up the heat and bring to the boil, then simmer gently for approximately 1½ hours until the chutney is thick but still juicy, stirring occasionally.

3 Remove the muslin bag, then pour the chutney into hot, sterilized jars (see page 8) and seal (see page 11).

hot tomato, apple, & chili chutney

As a variation on the previous recipe this version packs a punch—with the added oomph supplied by red hot chilies and a few extra spices. Delicious. Add a dollop to pasta.

For a hot tomato chutney with a chili kick, follow Red Tomato and Garlic Chutney, adding 3 deseeded and minced hot red chilies, and include 5 whole cardamom seeds with the spices and an extra couple of garlic cloves, if you wish.

Makes about 5 cups
2 pounds apples, peeled and cored
2½ cups cider vinegar
⅜ cup pickling spice
1 tbsp. ground ginger

1½ cups raisins
2 (packed) cups warmed brown sugar
   (see page 10)
2 tsp. salt
1 red chili, deseeded and minced (optional)

aunt edna's apple chutney

I was given this recipe in the 1970s by a friend's aunt and it was the first chutney I ever made. The results are totally reliable and since then I've made it many times. Thanks, Auntie Edna.

1 Place the apples and vinegar in a stainless steel preserving pan. Tie the pickling spice and ground ginger into a piece of cheesecloth with string and add to the pan. Cook gently until the apples are tender but still hold their shape.

2 Mince the raisins in a food processor, or chop roughly, and add them to the pan with the sugar, salt, and optional chili; mix well. Bring the chutney to the boil, cooking the mixture until thickened but still juicy, then remove from heat. Remove the spice bundle.

3 Pour the chutney into hot, sterilized jars (see page 8) and seal (see page 11).

Makes about 5 cups
2 pounds cooking apples, peeled, cored,
   and chopped
4½ cups malt vinegar
½ pound onions, peeled and chopped

2 scant tsp. mustard seeds
1 scant tsp. ground ginger
1½ scant cups warmed brown sugar (see
   page 10)
1¾ cups chopped dried dates
1 clove garlic, peeled and chopped

apple & date chutney

Every autumn I end up with bags of apples, even though I only possess one small crab apple tree. Friends always have more fruit than they can cope with so another recipe to use them up is great.

Place the first 5 ingredients in a stainless steel preserving pan, bring to the boil, then simmer until the apples are soft but still hold their shape. Remove from the heat and add the sugar, dates, and garlic, then stir over a gentle heat until the sugar is dissolved. Turn up the heat and bring to the boil, then simmer until the chutney is thick but still juicy. Pack as above.

Makes about 6½ cups

12 peppercorns

2 tsp. whole allspice

¾-inch-square piece of fresh gingerroot, bruised

5½ cups pumpkin flesh, cut into ⅝-inch cubes (from pumpkin weighing approx. 2¾ pounds)

1 pound cooking apples, peeled, cored, and finely chopped

2 rounded tbsp. minced stem ginger

¾ pound shallots, peeled, cored, and minced

1⅜ cup golden raisins, chopped

2 cloves garlic, minced

2 tsp. salt

2½ cups cider vinegar

1⅞ cups (packed) warmed soft brown sugar (see page 10)

pumpkin chutney

With their wonderful shapes, textures, and vibrant colors, pumpkins and squashes are always so visually appealing and their flesh gives this chutney a colorful look and sweeter flavor, which is always a good thing.

1 Place the dry spices and gingerroot in a piece of muslin and tie it into a bag with string. Place all the ingredients except the sugar in a stainless steel preserving pan and bring slowly to the boil, then simmer gently for 20 minutes until the pumpkin and apple are soft.

2 Add the warmed sugar and stir over a gentle heat until all the sugar has dissolved, then turn up the heat and simmer for approximately 1–1½ hours until the chutney is thick but still juicy, stirring occasionally.

3 Remove the muslin bag, then pour the chutney into hot, sterilized jars (see page 8) and seal (see page 11).

marrow squash chutney

It is great to find "good ways with marrow squash," since people who grow them always seem to end up with a glut of ginormous specimens but without a clue what to do with them. When it comes to preserving, and to chutneys in particular, marrow squash are a really useful "filler-outer," in the same way that apples are. However, they are a very watery vegetable, so you need to remove some of this liquid right at the start to concentrate the flavor.

Substitute the same amount of marrow squash for the pumpkin in Pumpkin Chutney. There is no need to add the stem ginger. Place the squash in a bowl, sprinkle with some salt, and leave for 12 hours to draw out the excess water; rinse thoroughly and drain, then follow the recipe above.

Makes about 5½ cups

3 pounds pears, peeled, cored, and cut
  into chunks
1 pound onions, peeled and chopped
grated rind and juice of 1 lemon
grated rind and juice of 1 orange
1 scant cup sugar
1½ scant cups seedless raisins
1¼ cups cider vinegar
1 tsp. salt
1 tsp. ground ginger
½ tsp. cloves

pear chutney

This chutney contains just the right combination of fruitiness and spiciness. I would always recommend that you leave chutney in the pantry for a couple of months before eating it; and although this pear chutney is no exception, it does taste remarkably good as soon as it is made. Keep it for a while if you can, otherwise devour and enjoy! It is great with cheese.

1 Place all the ingredients in a stainless steel preserving pan and stir over a gentle heat until all the sugar has dissolved. Bring to the boil, then simmer for approximately 2 hours until the chutney is dark and thick but still juicy, stirring occasionally. As with all chutneys, it will thicken up slightly as it cools.

2 Pour the chutney into hot, sterilized jars (see page 8) and seal (see page 11).

pickles

When it comes to pickles, vinegar is the star ingredient. Vinegar comes into its own here, and the more matured and spiced it is, the better. You can use any kind of vinegar but cider vinegar goes well with apples and pears, malt vinegar with darker pickles, and white wine vinegar helps the color of ingredients to be seen at their best.

Makes about 2¼ cups
2 pounds crab apples
2¾ cups cider or wine vinegar
1 small cinnamon stick

9 cloves
1 scant tsp allspice
3 cups warmed sugar (see page 10)

spiced crab apple pickle

The miniature nature of crab apples makes them very appealing and decorative when used whole, as they are in this pickle. Different varieties of apples will give a very different look to the pickle, and small ruby red apples look particularly cute.

Keep the apples whole and leave the stalks on, then allow a few pickled apples for each serving. The apples require so little preparation that this treatment is well suited to these otherwise awkward little fruits, but they do need to be in perfect condition before you start. You can use other apple varieties for this pickle if crab apples aren't available. Chop larger fruits, core them, and pickle the large chunks in the same way. This pickle is great served with cheese and biscuits.

1 Prick the apple skins with a darning needle.

2 Pour the vinegar into a stainless steel pan, add the spices and bring to the boil, then simmer for 5 minutes. Add the apples and simmer until they are tender but still hold their shape. Lift them carefully out of the vinegar, using a slotted spoon, and pack them into hot, sterilized jars (see page 8).

3 Add the warmed sugar to the vinegar and stir over a low heat until all the sugar has dissolved, then turn up the heat and boil steadily until the vinegar has reduced by about a third and become syrupy.

4 Pour the hot syrup over the apples so that it completely covers them and seal the jars (see page 11).

Makes about 3 cups
1 pint cider vinegar
2 cups sugar
juice and zest pared from 1 lemon, cut
    into chunks

5 whole allspice berries
2 star anise
2 dried red chilies
5 black peppercorns
3¼ pounds pears

pickled pears

This is such a lovely looking pickle. The pears are wonderful eaten as a relish with cold meats, and also work well with cheese. Use up any of the sweet, spiced vinegar remaining in the jar to make a salad dressing—drizzle it over a goat-cheese salad.

1 Place the vinegar, sugar, lemon peel pieces, and spices in a stainless steel pan and stir over a gentle heat to dissolve the sugar. Peel and quarter the pears and toss them in the lemon juice to prevent them from discoloring.

2 Place the pears in the spiced syrup and simmer gently for approximately 30 minutes until tender and translucent, depending on the ripeness of the fruit. Remove the pear pieces using a slotted spoon and place them in sterilized jars (see page 8).

3 Boil the syrup in the pan to reduce it by half, then pour the syrup and the spices over the pears, making sure they are completely covered. Leave until cold, then seal (see page 11).

Makes about 1¾ cups

3 plums, halved and stoned
2 apricots, halved and stoned
2 figs, halved
2 small pears, peeled and quartered

1¾ cups sugar
juice of 1 lemon
⅝ cup dry white wine
1 generous cup honey
½ cup (scant) English mustard powder

mostarda di frutta

If you are unfamiliar with mustard fruits, now is a good time to be introduced. It is a delicious mustard-based condiment with Italian origins. (The name actually comes not from "mustard" but from *mosto*, which is the unfermented grape juice, reduced to a thick syrup, in which the fruits were originally preserved.) Originally made with quinces or grapes, it can be made using any mixture of fruits—usually pears, plums, peaches, whole cherries, and figs.

This pickle can be served chopped over fish and goes well with pork and sausages and strong, salty cheeses. Finely chopped mostarda can also be mashed with pumpkin to make a filling for ravioli. Use any leftover syrup in salad dressings and drizzle over bitter salad leaves.

1 Preheat the oven to 250°F. Place all the fruit in a stainless steel pan and add just enough water to cover.

2 Add the sugar and lemon juice and stir gently to dissolve the sugar, then turn up the heat and boil to make a thin syrup. Simmer over low heat for about 10 minutes, so the fruit pieces are cooked but stay intact.

3 Remove the fruit pieces with a slotted spoon, draining them well, and place on a baking sheet. Cook in the oven for about 45–50 minutes until the fruits are dry.

4 Add the wine and honey to the syrup and simmer over low heat for 10–15 minutes to reduce it. Add the mustard powder and mix well.

5 Put the fruit pieces into hot, sterilized jars (see page 8) and pour the syrup over to cover. Leave until cold, then seal (see page 11).

Makes about 1¾ cups
1 pound damsons
1 scant cup sugar
2 short cinnamon sticks

6 cloves
4 pieces of gingerroot, about
  ¾-inch square
malt vinegar (for quantity see step 1)

pickled damsons

This traditional method for pickling damsons is well worth the effort. You could cut down the amount of straining and boiling, and you would still get a delicious pickle—if not quite as rich.

1 Preheat the oven to 300°F. Put the damson into a ceramic dish and sprinkle with sugar. Tie the spices in a piece of muslin. Pour enough vinegar onto the fruit to cover it, add the bag of spices, then put the dish at the bottom of the oven for 20 minutes until the fruits feel soft and the juices start to run.

2 Allow to cool, then strain the juice into a pan and add the spices. Bring to the boil, then discard the spices and pour the liquid over the damsons. Repeat this straining and boiling process (without spices) each day for 10 days, then leave the damsons immersed in the juice for another 7 days, refrigerating between processing.

3 Strain the damsons again and pack into a hot, sterilized jar (see page 8). Bring the rich, syrupy juice to the boil and pour over the damsons. Leave until cold, then seal the jar (see page 11).

Makes about 1¾ cups
1 pound apricots
1 scant cup sugar
2 short cinnamon sticks
2 cloves

2 pieces of gingerroot, about
  ¾-inch square
½ tsp whole allspice
wine vinegar (for quantity, see
  step 1 above)

pickled apricots

This is another versatile alternative, in which the sweetness of the fruit is perfectly offset by the sharpness of the vinegar. When apricots are out of season, use dried apricots instead.

Follow step 1 above, using the apricots and different spice quantities. Remove the apricots with a slotted spoon and pack into a sterilized jar (see page 8). Boil the remaining liquid until it becomes syrupy; discard the spice bag, then pour the liquid over the apricots. Leave in the refrigerator overnight. Next day, remove the apricots from the jar and strain the syrup into a pan. Put the apricots back in the jar and bring the syrup to the boil, then pour over the apricots. Leave until cold, then seal (see page 11).

Makes about 3 pints
8 or 9 small lemons
coarse salt (for quantity see step 2)
1 bay leaf

1 small cinnamon stick
a few coriander seeds
1 dried chili

preserved lemons

Preserved lemons are an essential ingredient in Moroccan and North African cuisines. They can be added to casseroles and salads and have a fragrant, sweet and sour taste. Once pickled, the whole fruit, rind and all, can be eaten. As the lemons are used, simply add more salt and lemon juice to the jar so the fruits stay immersed.

1 Cut off the stalk end of each lemon; then, holding it upright, slice it down in quarters to within ¾ inch of the base so it opens out but doesn't come apart.

2 Pack the salt in between the cuts, using approximately 1 tablespoonful for each lemon, then pack the lemons as tightly as you can into a large (approximately 1 quart), sterilized wide-necked jar (see page 8), pushing them down to encourage them to release their juice. Distribute the other flavorings (left whole) among the lemons. Close the jar and leave it overnight.

3 The next day, press the lemons down more so they release more juice. Continue doing this each day for the next 3 days until the lemons are completely submerged in the juice, adding more lemon juice if necessary.

4 Seal the jar (see page 11). Leave the lemons for 1 month, by which time they should be soft and ready to use.

5 Store the lemons in the refrigerator, where they will keep for at least 6 months. Rinse off excess salt before using.

Makes about 7 cups

1 pound cauliflower, broken into florets
½ pound scarlet runner beans, trimmed
½ pound green tomatoes, cut into chunks
1 pound shallots, peeled and halved if
 small
6 cups diced marrow squash flesh
⅞ cup salt

6¾ cups malt vinegar
⅞ cup sugar
1 rounded tbsp English mustard powder
2 tsp mustard seeds
1 tsp ground ginger
4 small dried chilies, crushed
¼ rounded cup cornstarch
2 tbsp turmeric

piccalilli

Piccalilli is a good way of preserving homegrown seasonal vegetables, and the medley can be changed to suit what you have available at the time. It is another resourceful way of using up marrow squash; or you can substitute zucchini—both crops that often fit into the "feast or famine" category; when available, there is usually an overabundance.

1 Mix all the vegetables together and layer them in a bowl, sprinkling salt in between the layers, then leave overnight. The next day, drain the vegetables, rinse thoroughly to remove all the salt, and drain again.

2 Pour the vinegar into a pan and stir in the sugar, mustard powder and seeds, ginger, and dried chilies. Add the vegetables and simmer until just tender but still in chunks. You can choose the texture of pickle you like best by keeping the vegetables crunchy or cook till soft.

3 Blend the cornstarch and turmeric with a few tablespoons of vinegar from the pan and stir this into the mixture, then boil for 2–3 minutes.

4 Pour the piccalilli into hot, sterilized jars (see page 8) and leave until cold, then seal (see page 11).

Makes about 3 cups
2 pounds shallots
½ (rounded) cup salt

2⅓ cups pickling vinegar
(see page 13)

pickled shallots

Pickled onions are a classic British pickle and one that seems to be popular with children and adults alike. They go with just about anything, but a simple lunch made up of a piece of crusty bread, a wedge of sharp cheese, and some pickled onions is a combination that is hard to beat. In order for your onions to retain that initial crunch, they need to be marinated in brine for a few days before being packed into jars and covered in spiced vinegar. Apart from that, this pickle has to be the easiest there is, and you should always keep a few jars on the pantry shelf.

1 Place the shallots in a large bowl without skinning them. Make the brine by dissolving half of the salt in 1 quart water, then pour this over the shallots and leave for 12 hours. Drain and skin the shallots.

2 Make a second batch of brine using the remaining salt and the same amount of water, pour it over the shallots, and leave for another 2–3 days.

3 Meanwhile, if you don't already have some pickling vinegar steeping in a cabinet, make a batch of the quick version a while before the brining period is due to finish; leave this until cold.

4 Drain and rinse the salt from the onions and pack them tightly into sterilized jars (see page 8). Pour the cold pickling vinegar over them so that they are completely covered. Cover and seal the jars (see page 11). The shallots will keep their flavor and crispness for up to 6 months after bottling.

sweet & sour onions

This pickle benefits from a sweeter vinegar than is used for the previous recipe, to give a delectable sweet and sour tang. It is very easy to make.

Here the onions are pickled in a sweet pickling vinegar. Follow the recipe above, but either use some sweet pickling vinegar already steeping in a cupboard or make up a batch of the quicker alternative instead (see page 13 for both recipes).

useful addresses

Many local hardware stores and well-stocked cook stores sell all the bits and pieces you need for jam making, from preserving pans to jars and labels. Here are a few online companies that also stock the things you will need:

www.allamericancanner.com
www.canningpantry.com
www.freshpreserving.com
www.kitchenkrafts.com

author's acknowledgments

Thanks to Sue Rowlands for bringing order to the proceedings, not to mention lovely props, a fabulous eye for detail, and general encouragement and friendship.

Thanks also to Cindy Richards for giving me the opportunity to write a book on a subject I love, as well the rest of the CICO team; Sally Powell and Gillian Haslam for patiently pulling it all together, Alison Bolus and Eleanor Van Zandt for making sense of it all, and Jane Smith for her lovely drawings.

Thanks to Deborah Schneebeli-Morrell for making white currant and chili jam using her own homegrown fruit, and to friends and neighbors for their help and support, especially Judy Dann for our foodie conversations and for sending me surprise recipes in the post on many occasions.

Thanks to the customers of my company, The Laundry (www.thelaundry.co.uk), for being understanding when I was distracted by thoughts of jam!

Finally, a massive thank you to Chris and Lisa for helping me keep life on an even keel so I could get on with the book, and to my friend, Lindsey Stock, without whose help the book would not have been possible.

index